CHRIST'S
40
COMMANDMENTS

COMPILED BY
RENEE VALVERDE WAGENBLATT

WESTBOW
PRESS®
A DIVISION OF THOMAS NELSON
& ZONDERVAN

WestBow Press books may be ordered through booksellers or by contacting:

WestBow Press
A Division of Thomas Nelson & Zondervan
1663 Liberty Drive
Bloomington, IN 47403
www.westbowpress.com
1 (866) 928-1240

Because of the dynamic nature of the Internet, any web addresses or
links contained in this book may have changed since publication and
may no longer be valid. The views expressed in this work are solely those
of the author and do not necessarily reflect the views of the publisher,
and the publisher hereby disclaims any responsibility for them.

Any people depicted in stock imagery provided by Thinkstock are
models, and such images are being used for illustrative purposes only.
Certain stock imagery © Thinkstock.

ISBN: 978-1-4908-8151-5 (sc)
ISBN: 978-1-4908-8153-9 (hc)
ISBN: 978-1-4908-8152-2 (e)

Library of Congress Control Number: 2015908319

Print information available on the last page.

WestBow Press rev. date: 1/4/2016

This book is dedicated to
my Savior Jesus Christ

PREFACE

I have read and used the English translation of the ancient biblical text as it is found in the New International Version of the Bible. Since I wished to extract the words of instruction given by Jesus Christ, I focused on the Gospels, the first four books of the New Testament: Matthew (Mt), Mark (Mk), Luke (Lk) and John (Jn). These are the books of the Bible that narrate the life of Jesus and preserve the record of his words of instruction.

Every time Jesus gave an instruction or commandment within the Gospels, I recorded it. By my count there are forty of these commandments. All forty can be found in Matthew. Christ states that two of the commandments are the greatest. Actually, in my opinion the entire Gospel message can be reduced to one word – love. This information is located in the next few pages and takes only a moment to read.

For those who hope to find more than two commandments, there is an alphabetical list of the forty commandments. This is followed by a list of one representative verse from Matthew for each commandment. An alphabetical list of each commandment with associated verses found in the four Gospels comprises the bulk of this text. It is more inclusive than a word search since it includes associated key words. I also noted some of Christ's exemplary behavior. Occasionally, I have included an adjacent verse to give clarification. Some verses quoted are used in more than one commandment category. Additional related material can be found in the appendices of this book. Of course, the full meaning can best be learned by reading the chapters found in the four Gospels of the Bible.

In this book I reiterate the words of Christ. I am not a scripture scholar but merely the compiler of what has been recorded. Now that I have identified Christ's forty commandments as I list them, I try to live by them and want to share them with you. Having prepared candidates for twenty-one years to succeed on national collegiate entrance tests, I am now focused on preparing others to succeed on the entrance test to Heaven. Jesus states in Jn 14:15, "If you love me, keep my commands." This document, which uses the form of a listing, is designed as a reference tool for everyone in a fast-paced world. I hope you find this book rewarding.

USE OF THIS BOOK

The distinction needs to be made between the record of God's commandments and the record of Christ's commandments. According to the Old Testament books of Exodus and Deuteronomy, God delivered Ten Commandments that were given to Moses. In subsequent years, Jewish law created numerous complex rules of living. In his message, Christ focused on the spiritual matters. Christ only rarely repeated verbatim any of God's commandments, but in Matthew's Gospel (Mt 19:17) he does state, "Keep the commandments." The body of this text is a listing of the verses associated with the forty commandments of Christ. God's Ten Commandments and the annotated concordance of the related verses are in Appendix A in the back of this book.

To use this book, go to page 8 titled "Forty Commands Alphabetically" in the front of this book and locate a commandment in the alphabetical list. Note the number to the left of the commandment. This is a chapter number. Find the associated verses for that commandment in the body of the text in alphabetical and numerical order.

EXAMPLES:

LOVE. Christ identifies three related commandments: love God, love neighbor, and love self. These are numbered 24, 25, & 26. To love God is both one of Christ's commandments and one of God's commandments. To love God is so essential that it is the only commandment that is listed in two places. The related verses are in the body of this text with Christ's commandments and repeated in Appendix A with God's commandments. The one complete message concerning love of God, neighbor, and self is titled "Two Greatest Commandments" in the front of this book on page 7.

DON'T STEAL. This is one of God's Ten Commandments so the related verses are in Appendix A in the back of the book.

PRAY / ASK. This is one of Christ's commandments. In the front of this book on page 8 is a numerical list titled "Forty Commands Alphabetically." PRAY / ASK is chapter 29.

NOTES:

In this text, the pronouns he, him, I and me all refer to Jesus unless otherwise noted in parenthesis. The referent of they or them as well as information beyond the scope of the verse is defined in the parenthesis at the end of the verse.

When [...] is placed at the beginning of a verse, it indicates to read the preceding verse. When [...] is placed at the end of a verse, it indicates to read the following verse.

Verses were copied from the NIV Bible. Some verses including quotes begin or end mid-sentence.

Mt 22:37 reads the Gospel of Matthew chapter 22 verse 37.

ABOUT THE AUTHOR

Renee Valverde Wagenblatt is a native of Kansas City, Missouri. Since she was a young student herself, she aided classmates to prepare for tests. She has taught various ages from preschool to seniors including teaching elementary a couple of years.

Renee Wagenblatt has a master's in adult education from the University of Missouri-Kansas City. Within the program she designed at UMKC titled Training for Entrance and Standardized Tests, she taught college, graduate and professional school candidates for twenty-one years. She is employed presently at the University of Oklahoma-Tulsa.

She holds office in a number of organizations. She enjoys being a lector at church as well as gathering with friends and family. She has traveled extensively including to biblical sites in Israel, Greece and Turkey.

A teacher at heart preparing individuals for tests, Renee wants to spread and teach Christ's word. Now her focal question is "Are you prepared for the entrance test to heaven?" It is her prayer that this book will assist the reader.

TABLE OF CONTENTS

Message Reduced to One Symbol..............................1
Message Reduced to One Word 3
Message Reduced to One Sentence 5
Two Greatest Commandments...............................7
40 Commands Alphabetically.................................8
40 Commands with One Verse 11
Additional Associated Keywords...........................19
40 Commands with Gospel Verses 25

APPENDICES

A. God's Ten Commandments.............................195
B. The Lord's Prayer..213
C. Instructions for Disciples 215
D. Blessed (Beatitudes)......................................221
E. Woes..225
F. Parables & Lessons 229
G. Miracles...235
H. Names Used In This Book 239

Index of Verse numbers 243
Commands by Category......................................268

MESSAGE REDUCED
TO ONE SYMBOL:

MESSAGE REDUCED TO ONE WORD:

LOVE

MESSAGE REDUCED
TO ONE SENTENCE:

LOVE GOD

THEN

YOUR NEIGHBOR

AS YOURSELF.

TWO GREATEST COMMANDMENTS

Mt 22:34	Hearing that Jesus had silenced the Sadducees, the Pharisees got together.
Mt 22:35	One of them, an expert in the law, tested him with this question:
Mt 22:36	"Teacher, which is the greatest commandment in the Law?"
Mt 22:37	1) Jesus replied: "'Love the Lord your God with all your heart and with all your soul and with all your mind.'
Mt 22:38	This is the first and greatest commandment.
Mt 22:39	2) And the second is like it: 'Love your neighbor as yourself.'
Mt 22:40	All the Law and the Prophets hang on these two commandments."

40 COMMANDS
ALPHABETICALLY

NO.		COMMAND
1.	DO	ACKNOWLEDGE JESUS
2.	DON'T	BE AFRAID
3.	DO	BEAR GOOD FRUIT
4.	DO	BEWARE / WATCH OUT
5.	DON'T	BLASPHEME
6.	DON'T	CAUSE OTHERS TO SIN
7.	DO	BE CHASTE
8.	DO	HAVE GOOD CONDUCT
9.	DO	DENY SELF / LEAVE TIES
10.	DON'T	DIVORCE
11.	DO	ELIMINATE IF BAD
12.	DO	ACT CONCERNING END TIMES
13.	DO	ENTER BY NARROW GATE
14.	DO	HAVE FAITH / BELIEVE
15.	DO	FOLLOW / COME
16.	DO	FORGIVE / SHOW MERCY
17.	DO	GOOD DEEDS / RIGHTEOUS
18.	DO	BE HUMBLE / MEEK

19.	DON'T	<u>JUDGE</u> / CONDEMN
20.	DO	HAVE RIGHT <u>JUDGEMENT</u>
21.	DO	<u>KEEP</u> THE COMMANDMENTS
22.	DO	<u>LEARN</u>
23.	DO	<u>LISTEN</u>/ACT ON GOD'S WORD
24.	DO	<u>LOVE</u> GOD / JESUS
25.	DO	<u>LOVE</u> YOUR NEIGHBOR
26.	DO	<u>LOVE</u> YOURSELF
27.	DO	ACCEPT <u>PERSECUTION</u>
28.	DO	<u>PERSEVERE</u>
29.	DO	<u>PRAY</u> / ASK
30.	DO	<u>PREPARE</u> / KEEP WATCH
31.	DO	<u>REBUKE</u> WRONGDOERS
32.	DO	<u>REPENT</u> / BE RECONCILED
33.	DO	REGARDING <u>SACRAMENTS</u>
34.	DO	BE A GOOD <u>SERVANT</u> / SLAVE
35.	DO	PROPER <u>SPEECH</u> / THOUGHTS
36.	DO	<u>TEACH</u> / PREACH
37.	DO	GIVE <u>THANKS</u> / ASK BLESSING
38.	DO	<u>TREAT THINGS</u> RESPECTFULLY
39.	DO	GOD'S <u>WILL</u>
40.	DON'T	<u>WORRY</u>

40 COMMANDS
WITH ONE VERSE

1. Mt 10:32   DO <u>ACKNOWLEDGE</u> JESUS
   "Whoever acknowledges me before others, I will also acknowledge before my Father in heaven.

2. Mt 10:28   DON'T BE <u>AFRAID</u>
   Do not be afraid of those who kill the body but cannot kill the soul. Rather, be afraid of the One who can destroy both soul and body in hell.

3. Mt 21:43   DO <u>BEAR</u> GOOD FRUIT
   "Therefore I tell you that the kingdom of God will be taken away from you and given to a people who will produce its fruit.

4. Mt 7:15   DO <u>BEWARE</u>
   "Watch out for false prophets. They come to you in sheep's clothing, but inwardly they are ferocious wolves.

5.   Mt 12:31   DON'T <u>BLASPHEME</u>
And so I tell you, every kind of sin and slander can be forgiven, but blasphemy against the Spirit will not be forgiven.

6.   Mt 18:6   DON'T <u>CAUSE</u> OTHERS TO SIN
"If anyone causes one of these little ones—those who believe in me—to stumble, it would be better for them to have a large millstone hung around their neck and to be drowned in the depths of the sea.

7.   Mt 15:19   DO BE <u>CHASTE</u>
For out of the heart come evil thoughts—murder, adultery, sexual immorality, theft, false testimony, slander.

8.   Mt 16:27   DO HAVE GOOD <u>CONDUCT</u>
For the Son of Man is going to come in his Father's glory with his angels, and then he will reward each person according to what they have done.

9.   Mt 16:24   DO <u>DENY</u> SELF / LEAVE TIES
Then Jesus said to his disciples, "Whoever wants to be my disciple must deny themselves and take up their cross and follow me.

10. Mt 19:6   DON'T <u>DIVORCE</u>
So they* are no longer two, but one flesh. Therefore what God has joined together, let no one separate." *(a man and wife)

11. Mt 18:8   DO <u>ELIMINATE</u> IF BAD
If your hand or your foot causes you to stumble, cut it off and throw it away. It is better for you to enter life maimed or crippled than to have two hands or two feet and be thrown into eternal fire.

12. Mt 24:4   DO ACT CONCERNING <u>END</u> TIMES
Jesus answered: "Watch out that no one deceives you.

13. Mt 7:13   DO <u>ENTER</u> BY NARROW GATE
"Enter through the narrow gate. For wide is the gate and broad is the road that leads to destruction, and many enter through it.

14. Mt 21:21   DO HAVE <u>FAITH</u>/BELIEVE
Jesus replied, "Truly I tell you, if you have faith and do not doubt, not only can you do what was done to the fig tree, but also you can say to this mountain, 'Go, throw yourself into the sea,' and it will be done.

15. Mt 10:38   DO <u>FOLLOW</u>/COME
Whoever does not take up their cross and follow me is not worthy of me.

16. Mt 6:14   DO <u>FORGIVE</u>/HAVE MERCY
For if you forgive other people when they
sin against you, your heavenly Father will
also forgive you.

17. Mt 6:20   DO <u>GOOD DEEDS</u>/RIGHTEOUS
But store up for yourselves treasures in
heaven, where moths and vermin do not
destroy, and where thieves do not break in
and steal.

18. Mt 18:4   DO BE <u>HUMBLE</u>/MEEK
Therefore, whoever takes the lowly position
of this child is the greatest in the kingdom
of heaven.

19. Mt 7:1   DON'T <u>JUDGE</u>/CONDEMN
"Do not judge, or you too will be judged.

20. Mt 23:23   DO HAVE RIGHT <u>JUDGMENT</u>
"Woe to you, teachers of the law and
Pharisees, you hypocrites! You give a tenth
of your spices—mint, dill and cumin. But
you have neglected the more important
matters of the law—justice, mercy and
faithfulness. You should have practiced the
latter, without neglecting the former.

21. Mt 19:17   DO <u>KEEP THE COMMANDMENTS</u>
"Why do you ask me about what is good?" Jesus replied. "There is only One who is good. If you want to enter life, keep the commandments."

22. Mt 11:29   DO <u>LEARN</u>
Take my yoke upon you and learn from me, for I am gentle and humble in heart, and you will find rest for your souls.

23. Mt 7:24   DO <u>LISTEN</u>/ACT ON GOD'S WORD
"Therefore everyone who hears these words of mine and puts them into practice is like a wise man who built his house on the rock.

24. Mt 22:37   DO <u>LOVE GOD/JESUS</u>
Jesus replied: "'Love the Lord your God with all your heart and with all your soul and with all your mind.'

25. Mt 5:44   DO <u>LOVE YOUR NEIGHBOR</u>
But I tell you, love your enemies and pray for those who persecute you,

26. Mt 22:39   DO <u>LOVE YOURSELF</u>
And the second* is like it: 'Love your neighbor as yourself.' *(commandment)

27. Mt 16:25   DO ACCEPT <u>PERSECUTION</u>
For whoever wants to save their life will lose it, but whoever loses their life for me will find it.

28. Mt 24:13   DO <u>PERSEVERE</u>
but the one who stands firm to the end will be saved.

29. Mt 6:9   DO <u>PRAY</u>/ASK
"This, then, is how you should pray: "'Our Father in heaven, hallowed be your name,

30. Mt 24:44   DO <u>PREPARE</u>/KEEP WATCH
So you also must be ready, because the Son of Man will come at an hour when you do not expect him.

31. Mt 7:5   DO <u>REBUKE</u> WRONGDOERS
You hypocrite, first take the plank out of your own eye, and then you will see clearly to remove the speck from your brother's eye.

32. Mt 4:17   DO <u>REPENT</u>/BE RECONCILED
From that time on Jesus began to preach, "Repent, for the kingdom of heaven has come near."

33. Mt 26:26   DO REGARDING <u>SACRAMENTS</u>
While they were eating, Jesus took bread, and when he had given thanks, he broke it and gave it to his disciples, saying, "Take and eat; this is my body."

34. Mt 23:11   DO BE A GOOD <u>SERVANT</u>/SLAVE
The greatest among you will be your servant.

35. Mt 12:37   DO PROPER <u>SPEECH</u>/THOUGHTS
For by your words you will be acquitted, and by your words you will be condemned."

36. Mt 28:20   DO <u>TEACH</u>/PREACH
and teaching them to obey everything I have commanded you. And surely I am with you always, to the very end of the age."

37. Mt 15:36   DO GIVE <u>THANKS</u>/ASK BLESSING
Then he took the seven loaves and the fish, and when he had given thanks, he broke them and gave them to the disciples, and they in turn to the people.

38. Mt 7:6   DO <u>TREAT THINGS</u> RESPECTFULLY
"Do not give dogs what is sacred; do not throw your pearls to pigs. If you do, they may trample them under their feet, and turn and tear you to pieces.

39.   Mt 7:21   DO GOD'S <u>WILL</u>

"Not everyone who says to me, 'Lord, Lord,' will enter the kingdom of heaven, but only the one who does the will of my Father who is in heaven.

40.   Mt 6:34   DON'T <u>WORRY</u>

Therefore do not worry about tomorrow, for tomorrow will worry about itself. Each day has enough trouble of its own.

ADDITIONAL ASSOCIATED KEYWORDS

1. DO <u>ACKNOWLEDGE</u> JESUS
   ashamed / disown / reject / well pleased

2. DON'T BE <u>AFRAID</u>
   alarmed / doubt / fear / frightened / peace / take courage / troubled

3. DO <u>BEAR</u> GOOD FRUIT
   produce / yield a crop

4. DO <u>BEWARE</u> / WATCH OUT
   be careful / on your guard

5. DON'T <u>BLASPHEME</u>
   speak against / stumble

6. DON'T <u>CAUSE</u> OTHERS TO SIN
   cause to stumble

7. DO BE <u>CHASTE</u>
   pure / sexual immorality

8. DO HAVE GOOD <u>CONDUCT</u>

   angry / comes out of a person / did for one / divided / do everything the authorities tell you / grumbling / have done / have salt / light within / perfect / set an example / stop sinning / take up cross / vineyard

9. DO <u>DENY</u> SELF/ LEAVE TIES

   bury father / don't have excess / drunkenness / fasting / give up / greed / hate self / left / look back / possessions / rich / self-indulgence / sell everything / sold / store up / treasures / wealth

10. DON'T <u>DIVORCE</u>

    separate

11. DO <u>ELIMINATE</u> IF BAD

    cause to stumble / cut down / take out

12. DO ACT CONCERNING <u>END</u> TIMES

13. DO <u>ENTER</u> BY NARROW GATE

    become like children / does will / I am the way / righteousness surpases / walk in light

14. DO HAVE <u>FAITH</u>/BELIEVE

    accepts / faithfullness / fall away / know God / know the truth

15. DO <u>FOLLOW</u>/COME

    do as I have done for you / showing yourselves to be my disciples / take my yoke upon you

16. DO <u>FORGIVE</u>/HAVE MERCY
    loose on earth / save the lost

17. DO <u>GOOD DEEDS</u>/RIGHTEOUS
    bless / did for one / do to others / store for yourselves
    treasures in heaven

18. DO BE <u>HUMBLE</u>/MEEK
    arrogance / like children

19. DON'T <u>JUDGE</u>/CONDEMN
    judge

20. DO HAVE RIGHT <u>JUDGMENT</u>
    justice

21. DO <u>KEEP THE COMMANDMENTS</u>
    do what I say / done everything told to do / faithfulness /
    hold to my teaching / know the truth / obey / practices /
    word that comes from God

22. DO <u>LEARN</u>
    these things happening

23. DO <u>LISTEN</u> / ACT ON GOD'S WORD
    hold my teaching / glorify / live on word / put into practice
    / reject / retain / understand / glorify / seek his kingdom
    / serve

24. DO <u>LOVE GOD / JESUS</u>
    command my spirit / don't be called master / don't test God / entrusted / give to God / glorify /honor / measure you use / praise / seek his kingdom / serve / stumble / worship

25. DO <u>LOVE YOUR NEIGHBOR</u>
    accept / angry / be generous / bless / despise / did for me / do as I have done / do not hinder / do to others / evils / give to others / hand over / invite / lend / measure you use / mercy / not as world gives / receives / serve / turn to them / weep / welcome

26. DO <u>LOVE YOURSELF</u>
    light within

27. DO ACCEPT <u>PERSECUTION</u>
    lay down his life / loses life your my sake

28. DO <u>PERSEVERE</u>
    audacity / fall away / keep putting them off / not give up / remain / salt among yourselves / stand firm to end

29. DO <u>PRAY</u>/ASK
    (Jesus prayers as examples)

30. DO <u>PREPARE</u>/WATCH
    be ready / be alert / watch

31. DO <u>REBUKE</u> WRONGDOERS
    (how to rebuke)

32. DO REPENT/RECONCILE
     (how to repent) / repentance / settle matters

33. DO REGARDING SACRAMENTS
     baptize / bind-loose / bread-cup / eat-drink / food that
     endures / Spirit

34. DO BE A GOOD SERVANT/SLAVE
     serve

35. DO PROPER SPEECH/THOUGHTS
     defend / false testimony / grumbling / mouth / praise / says
     / slander / speak / spoken / swear / what to say / words

36. DO TEACH/PREACH
     hear him / instructing / proclaiming / sending you / speak
     / spoke / stood up to read / strengthen / taught / tell them
     / testify

37. DO GIVE THANKS/ASK BLESSING
     praise (also see Ch. 24) / rejoice

38. DO TREAT THINGS RESPECTFULLY
     don't mistreat things / overturned tables / trusted

39. DO GOD'S WILL
     Father / to please him who sent me

40. DON'T WORRY
     anxieties / troubled / worries

40 COMMANDS
WITH
GOSPEL VERSES

1. DO <u>ACKNOWLEDGE</u> JESUS

Mt 3:17   And a voice from heaven said, "This* is my Son, whom I love; with him I am well pleased." *(at baptism of Jesus)

Mt 10:32   "Whoever acknowledges me before others, I will also acknowledge before my Father in heaven.

Mt 10:33   But whoever disowns me before others, I will disown before my Father in heaven.

Mt 17:5   While he was still speaking, a bright cloud covered them,* and a voice from the cloud said, "This is my Son, whom I love; with him I am well pleased. Listen to him!" *(Jesus and others)

Mk 1:11   And a voice came from heaven:* "You are my Son, whom I love; with you I am well pleased." *(over Jesus)

Mk 1:24   "What do you want with us,* Jesus of Nazareth? Have you come to destroy us? I know who you are—the Holy One of God!" *(impure spirits)

Mk 3:11   Whenever the impure spirits saw him, they fell down before him and cried out, "You are the Son of God."

Mk 5:7   He* shouted at the top of his voice, "What do you want with me, Jesus, Son of the Most High God? In God's name don't torture me!" *(a man with an unclean spirit named Legion)

Mk 8:38	If anyone is ashamed of me and my words in this adulterous and sinful generation, the Son of Man will be ashamed of them when he comes in his Father's glory with the holy angels."
Mk 9:7	Then a cloud appeared and covered them,* and a voice came from the cloud: "This is my Son, whom I love. Listen to him!" *(Jesus and others)
Lk 3:21	When all the people were being baptized, Jesus was baptized too. And as he was praying, heaven was opened [...]
Lk 3:22	[...] and the Holy Spirit descended on him in bodily form like a dove. And a voice came from heaven: "You are my Son, whom I love; with you I am well pleased."
Lk 9:26	Whoever is ashamed of me and my words, the Son of Man will be ashamed of them when he comes in his glory and in the glory of the Father and of the holy angels.
Lk 9:35	A voice came from the cloud, saying, "This is my Son, whom I have chosen; listen to him."
Lk 10:16	"Whoever listens to you listens to me; whoever rejects you rejects me; but whoever rejects me rejects him who sent me."
Lk 12:8	"I tell you, whoever publicly acknowledges me before others, the Son of Man will also acknowledge before the angels of God. [...]
Lk 12:9	[...] But whoever disowns me before others will be disowned before the angels of God.

Jn 1:29

The next day John saw Jesus coming toward him and said, "Look, the Lamb of God, who takes away the sin of the world!

Jn 12:28

Father, glorify your name!" Then a voice came from heaven, "I have glorified it, and will glorify it again."

Jn 17:8

For I gave them* the words you** gave me and they accepted them. They knew with certainty that I came from you, and they believed that you sent me. *(those in the world given by God to Jesus) **(God)

29

2. DON'T BE <u>AFRAID</u>

Mt 10:26   "So do not be afraid of them,* for there is nothing concealed that will not be disclosed, or hidden that will not be made known. *(those of the house of Beelzebul)

Mt 10:28   Do not be afraid of those who kill the body but cannot kill the soul. Rather, be afraid of the One who can destroy both soul and body in hell.

Mt 10:31   So don't be afraid; you are worth more than many sparrows.

Mt 14:27   But Jesus immediately said to them:* "Take courage! It is I. Don't be afraid." *(the disciples who saw him walking on water)

Mt 14:31   Immediately Jesus reached out his hand and caught him.* "You of little faith," he said, "why did you doubt?"** *(Peter) **(that Peter could walk on water if Jesus was there)

Mt 17:7   But Jesus came and touched them.* "Get up," he said. "Don't be afraid." *(the disciples)

Mt 24:6   You will hear of wars and rumors of wars, but see to it that you are not alarmed. Such things must happen, but the end is still to come.

Mt 28:10   Then Jesus said to them,* "Do not be afraid. Go and tell my brothers to go to Galilee; there they will see me." *(Mary Magdalene and the other Mary)

Mk 4:40   He said to his disciples,* "Why are you so afraid? Do you still have no faith?" *(during a storm at sea)

Mk 5:36   Overhearing what they* said,** Jesus told him,*** "Don't be afraid; just believe." *(people from the house of Jairus, the synagogue leader) **("Why bother the teacher anymore?" Since the man's daughter was already dead) ***(Jairus)

Mk 6:50   because they* all saw him** and were terrified.*** Immediately he spoke to them and said, "Take courage! It is I. Don't be afraid." *(the disciples) **(Jesus) ***(since he was walking on the water like a ghost)

Mk 13:7   When you hear of wars and rumors of wars, do not be alarmed. Such things must happen, but the end is still to come.

Lk 2:10   But the angel said to them,* "Do not be afraid. I bring you good news that will cause great joy for all the people. *(Shepherds near place of Jesus birth)

Lk 5:10   and so were* James and John, the sons of Zebedee, Simon's partners. Then Jesus said to Simon, "Don't be afraid; from now on you will fish for people." *(astonished at the large catch of fish)

Lk 8:49   While Jesus was still speaking, someone came from the house of Jairus, the synagogue leader. "Your daughter is dead," he said. "Don't bother the teacher anymore." [...]

Lk 8:50   [...] Hearing this,* Jesus said to Jairus, "Don't
               be afraid; just believe, and she will be healed."
               *(Lk 8:49)

Lk 12:4   "I tell you, my friends, do not be afraid of
               those who kill the body and after that can do
               no more.

Lk 12:5   But I will show you whom you should fear:
               Fear him who, after your body has been killed,
               has authority to throw you into hell. Yes, I tell
               you, fear him.

Lk 12:7   Indeed, the very hairs of your head are all
               numbered. Don't be afraid; you are worth
               more than many sparrows.

Lk 12:32   "Do not be afraid, little flock, for your Father
               has been pleased to give you the kingdom.

Lk 21:9   When you hear of wars and uprisings, do not
               be frightened. These things must happen first,
               but the end will not come right away."

Lk 24:36   While they* were still talking about this,**
               Jesus himself stood among them*** and said
               to them, "Peace be with you." *(two travelers)
               **(that Jesus was risen and earlier was
               recognized by some of them) ***(the eleven
               and those with them) [...]

Lk 24:38   [...] He said to them,* "Why are you troubled,
               and why do doubts rise in your minds? *(the
               eleven and those with them)

Jn 6:20   But he said to them,* "It is I; don't be afraid."
               *(the disciples)

Jn 14:27 Peace I leave with you; my peace I give you. I do not give to you as the world gives. Do not let your hearts be troubled and do not be afraid.

Jn 16:33 "I have told you these things,* so that in me you may have peace. In this world you will have trouble. But take heart! I have overcome the world." *(the disciples will be scattered and that the Father is with Jesus)

Jn 20:19 On the evening of that first day of the week, when the disciples were together, with the doors locked for fear of the Jewish leaders, Jesus came and stood among them and said, "Peace be with you!"

Jn 20:21 Again Jesus said, "Peace be with you! As the Father has sent me, I am sending you."* *(the disciples)

Jn 20:26 A week later his disciples were in the house again, and Thomas was with them. Though the doors were locked, Jesus came and stood among them and said, "Peace be with you!"

3. DO **BEAR** GOOD FRUIT

Mt 7:19	Every tree that does not bear good fruit is cut down and thrown into the fire.
Mt 12:33	"Make a tree good and its fruit will be good, or make a tree bad and its fruit will be bad, for a tree is recognized by its fruit.
Mt 13:8	Still other seed fell on good soil, where it produced a crop—a hundred, sixty or thirty times what was sown. [...]
Mt 13:23	[...] But the seed falling on good soil refers to someone who hears the word and understands it. This is the one who produces a crop, yielding a hundred, sixty or thirty times what was sown."
Mt 21:43	"Therefore I tell you that the kingdom of God will be taken away from you and given to a people who will produce its fruit.
Mk 4:8	Still other seed fell on good soil. It came up, grew and produced a crop, some multiplying thirty, some sixty, some a hundred times." [...]
Mk 4:9	[...] Then Jesus said, "Whoever has ears to hear, let them hear." [...]
Mk 4:20	[...] Others, like seed sown on good soil, hear the word, accept it, and produce a crop—some thirty, some sixty, some a hundred times what was sown."

Lk 8:8	Still other seed fell on good soil. It came up and yielded a crop, a hundred times more than was sown." When he said this, he called out, "Whoever has ears to hear, let them hear." [...]
Lk 8:15	[...] But the seed on good soil stands for those with a noble and good heart, who hear the word, retain it, and by persevering produce a crop.
Lk 13:8	"'Sir,'* the man** replied, 'leave it*** alone for one more year, and I'll dig around it and fertilize it. *(the orchard owner) **(the gardener) ***(a non-producing fig tree) [...]
Lk 13:9	[...] If it* bears fruit next year, fine! If not, then cut it down.'" *(a non-producing fig tree)
Jn 12:24	Very truly I tell you, unless a kernel of wheat falls to the ground and dies, it remains only a single seed. But if it dies, it produces many seeds.
Jn 15:4	Remain in me, as I also remain in you. No branch can bear fruit by itself; it must remain in the vine. Neither can you bear fruit unless you remain in me.
Jn 15:5	"I am the vine; you are the branches. If you remain in me and I in you, you will bear much fruit; apart from me you can do nothing.
Jn 15:8	This is to my Father's glory, that you bear much fruit, showing yourselves to be my disciples.
Jn 15:16	You did not choose me, but I chose you and appointed you so that you might go and bear fruit—fruit that will last—and so that whatever you ask in my name the Father will give you.

4. BEWARE / WATCH OUT

Mt 7:15	"Watch out for false prophets. They come to you in sheep's clothing, but inwardly they are ferocious wolves.
Mt 10:16	"I am sending you out like sheep among wolves. Therefore be as shrewd as snakes and as innocent as doves. [...]
Mt 10:17	[...] Be on your guard; you will be handed over to the local councils and be flogged in the synagogues.
Mt 16:6	"Be careful," Jesus said to them.* "Be on your guard against the yeast of the Pharisees and Sadducees." *(the disciples) [...]
Mt 16:11	[...] How is it you don't understand that I was not talking to you about bread? But be on your guard against the yeast of the Pharisees and Sadducees." [...]
Mt 16:12	[...] Then they* understood that he was not telling them to guard against the yeast used in bread, but against the teaching of the Pharisees and Sadducees. *(the disciples)
Mt 24:4	Jesus answered:* "Watch out that no one deceives you. *(to the disciples regarding when and how the end would be)
Mk 8:15	"Be careful," Jesus warned them.* "Watch out for the yeast of the Pharisees and that of Herod." *(the disciples)

Mk 12:38	As he taught, Jesus said, "Watch out for the teachers of the law. They like to walk around in flowing robes and be greeted with respect in the marketplaces, [...]
Mk 12:39	[...] and have the most important seats in the synagogues and the places of honor at banquets. [...]
Mk 12:40	[...] They* devour widows' houses and for a show make lengthy prayers. These men will be punished most severely." *(teachers of the law)
Mk 13:5	Jesus said to them:* "Watch out that no one deceives you. *(Peter, James, John and Andrew)
Mk 13:9	"You must be on your guard. You will be handed over to the local councils and flogged in the synagogues. On account of me you will stand before governors and kings as witnesses to them.
Mk 13:23	So be on your guard; I have told you everything ahead of time.
Mk 13:33	Be on guard! Be alert! You do not know when that time will come.
Lk 12:1	Meanwhile, when a crowd of many thousands had gathered, so that they were trampling on one another, Jesus began to speak first to his disciples, saying: "Be on your guard against the yeast of the Pharisees, which is hypocrisy.
Lk 12:15	Then he said to them, "Watch out! Be on your guard against all kinds of greed; life does not consist in an abundance of possessions."

Lk 20:46	"Beware of the teachers of the law. They like to walk around in flowing robes and love to be greeted with respect in the marketplaces and have the most important seats in the synagogues and the places of honor at banquets.
Lk 21:8	He replied: "Watch out that you are not deceived. For many will come in my name, claiming, 'I am he,' and, 'The time is near.' Do not follow them.
Lk 21:34	"Be careful, or your hearts will be weighed down with carousing, drunkenness and the anxieties of life, and that day will close on you suddenly like a trap. [...]
Lk 21:35	[...] For it will come on all those who live on the face of the whole earth.
Lk 21:36	Be always on the watch, and pray that you may be able to escape all that is about to happen, and that you may be able to stand before the Son of Man."

5. DON'T BLASPHEME

Mt 12:31	And so I tell you, every kind of sin and slander can be forgiven, but blasphemy against the Spirit will not be forgiven.
Mt 12:32	Anyone who speaks a word against the Son of Man will be forgiven, but anyone who speaks against the Holy Spirit will not be forgiven, either in this age or in the age to come.
Mk 3:28	Truly I tell you, people can be forgiven all their sins and every slander they utter, [...]
Mk 3:29	[...] but whoever blasphemes against the Holy Spirit will never be forgiven; they are guilty of an eternal sin."
Lk 7:23	Blessed is anyone who does not stumble on account of me."
Lk 12:10	And everyone who speaks a word against the Son of Man will be forgiven, but anyone who blasphemes against the Holy Spirit will not be forgiven.

6. DON'T <u>CAUSE</u> OTHERS TO SIN

Mt 18:6   "If anyone causes one of these little ones—
those who believe in me—to stumble, it would
be better for them to have a large millstone
hung around their neck and to be drowned in
the depths of the sea.

Mt 18:7   Woe to the world because of the things that
cause people to stumble! Such things must
come, but woe to the person through whom
they come!

Mk 9:42   "If anyone causes one of these little ones—
those who believe in me—to stumble, it would
be better for them if a large millstone were
hung around their neck and they were thrown
into the sea.

Lk 17:1   Jesus said to his disciples: "Things that cause
people to stumble are bound to come, but woe
to anyone through whom they come. [...]

Lk 17:2   [...] It would be better for them to be thrown
into the sea with a millstone tied around their
neck than to cause one of these little ones to
stumble.

7. DO BE <u>CHASTE</u>

Mt 5:8	Blessed are the pure in heart, for they will see God.
Mt 15:19	For out of the heart come evil thoughts—murder, adultery, sexual immorality, theft, false testimony, slander. [...]
Mt 15:20	[...] These* are what defile a person; but eating with unwashed hands does not defile them." *(Mt 15:19)
Mk 7:21	For it is from within, out of a person's heart, that evil thoughts come—sexual immorality, theft, murder, [...]
Mk 7:22	[...] adultery, greed, malice, deceit, lewdness, envy, slander, arrogance and folly. [...]
Mk 7:23	[...] All these* evils come from inside and defile a person." *(Mk 7:21 and Mk 7:22)

8. DO HAVE GOOD <u>CONDUCT</u>

Mt 5:22   But I tell you that anyone who is angry with a brother or sister will be subject to judgment. Again, anyone who says to a brother or sister, 'Raca,' is answerable to the court. And anyone who says, 'You fool!' will be in danger of the fire of hell.

Mt 5:48   Be perfect, therefore, as your heavenly Father is perfect.

Mt 10:38   Whoever does not take up their cross and follow me is not worthy of me.

Mt 15:19   For out of the heart come evil thoughts— murder, adultery, sexual immorality, theft, false testimony, slander. [...]

Mt 15:20   [...] These* are what defile a person; but eating with unwashed hands does not defile them." *(Mt 15:19)

Mt 16:24   Then Jesus said to his disciples, "Whoever wants to be my disciple must deny themselves and take up their cross and follow me.

Mt 16:27   For the Son of Man is going to come in his Father's glory with his angels, and then he will reward each person according to what they have done.

Mt 19:21	Jesus answered,* "If you want to be perfect, go, sell your possessions and give to the poor, and you will have treasure in heaven. Then come, follow me." *(a wealthy man with many possessions who had kept all of God's commandments)
Mt 23:3	So you must be careful to do everything they* tell you. But do not do what they do, for they do not practice what they preach. *(teachers of the law and Pharisees)
Mt 25:40	"The King* will reply, 'Truly I tell you,** whatever you did for one of the least of these brothers and sisters of mine, you did for me.' *(the Son of Man) **(the righteous on his right) [...]
Mt 25:45	[...] "He* will reply, 'Truly I tell you,** whatever you did not do for one of the least of these, you did not do for me.' *(the King - the Son of Man) **(the accursed on his left) [...]
Mt 25:46	[...] "Then they* will go away to eternal punishment, but the righteous** to eternal life." *(Mt 25:45) **(Mt 25:40)
Mk 7:14	Again Jesus called the crowd to him and said, "Listen to me, everyone, and understand this. [...]
Mk 7:15	[...] Nothing outside a person can defile them by going into them. Rather, it is what comes out of a person that defiles them."
Mk 7:21	For it is from within, out of a person's heart, that evil thoughts come—sexual immorality, theft, murder, [...]

Mk 7:22	[...] adultery, greed, malice, deceit, lewdness, envy, slander, arrogance and folly. [...]
Mk 7:23	[...] All these* evils come from inside and defile a person." *(Mk 7:21 and Mk 7:22)
Mk 8:34	Then he called the crowd to him along with his disciples and said: "Whoever wants to be my disciple must deny themselves and take up their cross and follow me.
Mk 9:50	"Salt is good, but if it loses its saltiness, how can you make it salty again? Have salt among yourselves, and be at peace with each other."
Mk 10:19	You know the commandments: 'You shall not murder, you shall not commit adultery, you shall not steal, you shall not give false testimony, you shall not defraud, honor your father and mother,'"
Mk 12:9	"What then will the owner of the vineyard do?* He will come and kill those tenants and give the vineyard to others. *(to those who did not observe the rules but rather beat and killed the ones who came for the fruit of the vineyard)
Lk 9:23	Then he said to them all: "Whoever wants to be my disciple must deny themselves and take up their cross daily and follow me.
Lk 11:17	Jesus knew their thoughts and said to them: "Any kingdom divided against itself will be ruined, and a house divided against itself will fall.
Lk 11:35	See to it, then, that the light within you is not darkness.

Lk 14:27	And whoever does not carry their cross and follow me cannot be my disciple.
Jn 5:14	Later Jesus found him* at the temple and said to him, "See, you are well again. Stop sinning or something worse may happen to you." *(the man who was healed and told to take up his mat and walk)
Jn 6:43	"Stop grumbling among yourselves,"* Jesus answered. *(some Jews)
Jn 8:34	Jesus replied,* "Very truly I tell you, everyone who sins is a slave to sin. *(to the Jews who believed in him)
Jn 13:15	I have set you an example that you should do as I have done for you.

9. DO <u>DENY</u> SELF / LEAVE TIES

Mt 4:2	After fasting forty days and forty nights, he was hungry.
Mt 6:16	"When you fast, do not look somber as the hypocrites do, for they disfigure their faces to show others they are fasting. Truly I tell you, they have received their reward in full.
Mt 6:17	But when you fast, put oil on your head and wash your face, [...]
Mt 6:18	[...] so that it will not be obvious to others that you are fasting, but only to your Father, who is unseen; and your Father, who sees what is done in secret, will reward you.
Mt 6:19	"Do not store up for yourselves treasures on earth, where moths and vermin destroy, and where thieves break in and steal.
Mt 6:20	But store up for yourselves treasures in heaven, where moths and vermin do not destroy, and where thieves do not break in and steal.
Mt 9:15	Jesus answered,* "How can the guests of the bridegroom mourn while he is with them? The time will come when the bridegroom will be taken from them;** then they will fast. *(the disciples of John) **(the disciples of Jesus)
Mt 13:22	The seed falling among the thorns refers to someone who hears the word, but the worries of this life and the deceitfulness of wealth choke the word, making it unfruitful.

Mt 13:44	"The kingdom of heaven is like treasure hidden in a field. When a man found it, he hid it again, and then in his joy went and sold all he had and bought that field.
Mt 13:45	"Again, the kingdom of heaven is like a merchant looking for fine pearls. [...]
Mt 13:46	[...] When he found one of great value, he went away and sold everything he had and bought it.
Mt 16:24	Then Jesus said to his disciples, "Whoever wants to be my disciple must deny themselves and take up their cross and follow me.
Mt 19:21	Jesus answered,* "If you want to be perfect, go, sell your possessions and give to the poor, and you will have treasure in heaven. Then come, follow me." *(a wealthy man with many possessions who had kept all of God's commandments) [...]
Mt 19:23	[...] Then Jesus said to his disciples, "Truly I tell you, it is hard for someone who is rich to enter the kingdom of heaven. [...]
Mt 19:24	[...] Again I tell you, it is easier for a camel to go through the eye of a needle than for someone who is rich to enter the kingdom of God."
Mt 19:29	And everyone who has left houses or brothers or sisters or father or mother or wife or children or fields for my sake will receive a hundred times as much and will inherit eternal life.
Mt 23:25	"Woe to you, teachers of the law and Pharisees, you hypocrites! You clean the outside of the cup and dish, but inside they are full of greed and self-indulgence.

Mk 2:20	But the time will come when the bridegroom will be taken from them,* and on that day they will fast.** *(guests of the bridegroom) **(comparison with Jesus and the disciples)
Mk 4:18	Still others, like seed sown among thorns, hear the word; [...]
Mk 4:19	[...] but the worries of this life, the deceitfulness of wealth and the desires for other things come in and choke the word, making it unfruitful.
Mk 7:21	For it is from within, out of a person's heart, that evil thoughts come—sexual immorality, theft, murder, [...]
Mk 7:22	[...] adultery, greed, malice, deceit, lewdness, envy, slander, arrogance and folly. [...]
Mk 7:23	[...] All these* evils come from inside and defile a person." *(Mk 7:21 and Mk 7:22)
Mk 8:34	Then he called the crowd to him along with his disciples and said: "Whoever wants to be my disciple must deny themselves and take up their cross and follow me.
Mk 10:21	Jesus looked at him* and loved him. "One thing you lack," he said. "Go, sell everything you have and give to the poor, and you will have treasure in heaven. Then come, follow me." *(a wealthy man who had kept all of God's commandments who wanted to know how to inherit eternal life) [...]
Mk 10:23	[...] Jesus looked around and said to his disciples, "How hard it is for the rich to enter the kingdom of God!" [...]

Mk 10:25   [...] It is easier for a camel to go through the eye of a needle than for someone who is rich to enter the kingdom of God."

Mk 10:29   "Truly I tell you," Jesus replied, "no one who has left home or brothers or sisters or mother or father or children or fields for me and the gospel [...]

Mk 10:30   [...] will fail to receive a hundred times as much in this present age: homes, brothers, sisters, mothers, children and fields—along with persecutions—and in the age to come eternal life.

Mk 12:44   They* all gave out of their wealth; but she,** out of her poverty, put in*** everything— all she had to live on." *(many rich people) **(a poor widow) ***(donating to the temple treasury)

Lk 2:37   and then was a widow* until she was eighty-four. She never left the temple but worshiped night and day, fasting and praying. *(Anna, a prophet)

Lk 5:35   But the time will come when the bridegroom will be taken from them;* in those days they will fast." *(Jesus' disciples)

Lk 9:23   Then he said to them all: "Whoever wants to be my disciple must deny themselves and take up their cross daily and follow me.

Lk 9:59   He said to another man, "Follow me." But he replied, "Lord, first let me go and bury my father." [...]

Lk 9:60	[...] Jesus said to him, "Let the dead bury their own dead, but you go and proclaim the kingdom of God."
Lk 9:61	Still another said, "I will follow you, Lord; but first let me go back and say goodbye to my family." [...]
Lk 9:62	[...] Jesus replied, "No one who puts a hand to the plow and looks back is fit for service in the kingdom of God."
Lk 12:15	Then he said to them, "Watch out! Be on your guard against all kinds of greed; life does not consist in an abundance of possessions."
Lk 12:21	"This* is how it will be with whoever stores up things for themselves but is not rich toward God." *(like a dying man who cannot take his possessions with him)
Lk 12:33	Sell your possessions and give to the poor. Provide purses for yourselves that will not wear out, a treasure in heaven that will never fail, where no thief comes near and no moth destroys.
Lk 14:26	"If anyone comes to me and does not hate father and mother, wife and children, brothers and sisters—yes, even their own life—such a person cannot be my disciple.
Lk 14:33	In the same way,* those of you who do not give up everything you have cannot be my disciples. *(as someone who builds a tower or marches into battle)

Lk 18:22	When Jesus heard this,* he said to him,** "You still lack one thing. Sell everything you have and give to the poor, and you will have treasure in heaven. Then come, follow me." *(the question of how one should inherit eternal life if he has obeyed all the commandments since his youth) **(a wealthy ruler)
Lk 18:24	[...] Jesus looked at him* and said, "How hard it is for the rich to enter the kingdom of God! *(the ruler now sad because he was very wealthy) [...]
Lk 18:25	[...] Indeed, it is easier for a camel to go through the eye of a needle than for someone who is rich to enter the kingdom of God."
Lk 18:29	"Truly I tell you," Jesus said to them, "no one who has left home or wife or brothers or sisters or parents or children for the sake of the kingdom of God [...]
Lk 18:30	[...] will fail to receive many times as much in this age, and in the age to come eternal life."
Lk 21:34	"Be careful, or your hearts will be weighed down with carousing, drunkenness and the anxieties of life, and that day will close on you suddenly like a trap. [...]
Lk 21:35	[...] For it will come on all those who live on the face of the whole earth

10. DON'T <u>DIVORCE</u>

Mt 5:32	But I tell you that anyone who divorces his wife, except for sexual immorality, makes her the victim of adultery, and anyone who marries a divorced woman commits adultery.
Mt 19:6	So they are no longer two, but one flesh. Therefore what God has joined together, let no one separate."
Mt 19:7	"Why then," they* asked, "did Moses command that a man give his wife a certificate of divorce and send her away?" *(the Pharisees) [...]
Mt 19:8	[...] Jesus replied, "Moses permitted you to divorce your wives because your hearts were hard. But it was not this way from the beginning.
Mt 19:9	I tell you that anyone who divorces his wife, except for sexual immorality, and marries another woman commits adultery."
Mk 10:9	Therefore what God has joined together, let no one separate."
Mk 10:11	He answered, "Anyone who divorces his wife and marries another woman commits adultery against her. [...]
Mk 10:12	[...] And if she* divorces her husband and marries another man, she commits adultery." *(a wife)
Lk 16:18	"Anyone who divorces his wife and marries another woman commits adultery, and the man who marries a divorced woman commits adultery.

11. DO <u>ELIMINATE</u> IF BAD

Mt 5:29   If your right eye causes you to stumble, gouge it out and throw it away. It is better for you to lose one part of your body than for your whole body to be thrown into hell.

Mt 5:30   And if your right hand causes you to stumble, cut it off and throw it away. It is better for you to lose one part of your body than for your whole body to go into hell.

Mt 7:5   You hypocrite, first take the plank out of your own eye, and then you will see clearly to remove the speck from your brother's eye.

Mt 7:19   Every tree that does not bear good fruit is cut down and thrown into the fire.

Mt 18:8   If your hand or your foot causes you to stumble, cut it off and throw it away. It is better for you to enter life maimed or crippled than to have two hands or two feet and be thrown into eternal fire.

Mt 18:9   And if your eye causes you to stumble, gouge it out and throw it away. It is better for you to enter life with one eye than to have two eyes and be thrown into the fire of hell.

Mk 9:43   If your hand causes you to stumble, cut it off. It is better for you to enter life maimed than with two hands to go into hell, where the fire never goes out.

Mk 9:45   And if your foot causes you to stumble, cut it off. It is better for you to enter life crippled than to have two feet and be thrown into hell.

Mk 9:47   And if your eye causes you to stumble, pluck it out. It is better for you to enter the kingdom of God with one eye than to have two eyes and be thrown into hell,

Lk 13:8   "'Sir,'* the man** replied, 'leave it*** alone for one more year, and I'll dig around it and fertilize it. *(the orchard owner) **(the gardener) ***(a non-producing fig tree) [...]

Lk 13:9   [...] If it* bears fruit next year, fine! If not, then cut it down.'" *(a non-producing fig tree)

12. DO ACT CONCERNING <u>END</u> TIMES

Mt 10:22	You will be hated by everyone because of me, but the one who stands firm to the end will be saved.
Mt 24:4	Jesus answered:* "Watch out that no one deceives you. *(to the disciples regarding when and how the end would be)
Mt 24:6	You will hear of wars and rumors of wars, but see to it that you are not alarmed. Such things must happen, but the end is still to come.
Mt 24:13	but the one who stands firm to the end will be saved.
Mt 24:15	"So when you see standing in the holy place 'the abomination that causes desolation,' spoken of through the prophet Daniel—let the reader understand—[...]
Mt 24:16	[...] then let those who are in Judea flee to the mountains. [...]
Mt 24:17	[...] Let no one on the housetop go down to take anything out of the house [...]
Mt 24:18	[...] Let no one in the field go back to get their cloak.
Mt 24:20	Pray that your flight will not take place in winter or on the Sabbath.
Mt 24:23	At that time if anyone says to you, 'Look, here is the Messiah!' or, 'There he is!' do not believe it.

Mt 24:26	"So if anyone tells you, 'There he is, out in the wilderness,' do not go out; or, 'Here he is, in the inner rooms,' do not believe it.
Mt 24:32	"Now learn this lesson from the fig tree: As soon as its twigs get tender and its leaves come out, you know that summer is near. [...]
Mt 24:33	[...] Even so, when you see all these things,* you know that it is near, right at the door. *(Mt 24:6 - Mt 24:26)
Mt 24:42	"Therefore keep watch, because you do not know on what day your Lord will come.
Mt 24:43	But understand this: If the owner of the house had known at what time of night the thief was coming, he would have kept watch and would not have let his house be broken into.[...]
Mt 24:44	[...]So you also must be ready, because the Son of Man will come at an hour when you do not expect him.
Mt 24:46	It will be good for that servant whose master finds him doing so* when he returns. *(being faithful)
Mt 24:50	The master of that servant* will come on a day when he does not expect him and at an hour he is not aware of. *(who beats fellow servants and eats with drunkards)
Mt 25:13	"Therefore keep watch, because you do not know the day or the hour.* *(of the coming of the Son of Man)
Mt 26:41	"Watch and pray so that you will not fall into temptation. The spirit is willing, but the flesh is weak."

Mk 13:4	"Tell us, when will these things* happen? And what will be the sign that they are all about to be fulfilled?" *(the end) [...]
Mk 13:5	[...] Jesus said to them:* "Watch out that no one deceives you. *(Peter, James, John and Andrew)
Mk 13:7	When you hear of wars and rumors of wars, do not be alarmed. Such things must happen, but the end is still to come.
Mk 13:9	"You must be on your guard. You will be handed over to the local councils and flogged in the synagogues. On account of me you will stand before governors and kings as witnesses to them.
Mk 13:11	Whenever you are arrested and brought to trial, do not worry beforehand about what to say. Just say whatever is given you at the time, for it is not you speaking, but the Holy Spirit.
Mk 13:13	Everyone will hate you because of me, but the one who stands firm to the end will be saved.
Mk 13:14	"When you see 'the abomination that causes desolation' standing where it does not belong—let the reader understand—then let those who are in Judea flee to the mountains. [...]
Mk 13:15	[...] Let no one on the housetop go down or enter the house to take anything out. [...]
Mk 13:16	[...] Let no one in the field go back to get their cloak.
Mk 13:18	Pray that this* will not take place in winter, *(the end)

Mk 13:21	At that time* if anyone says to you, 'Look, here is the Messiah!' or, 'Look, there he is!' do not believe it. *(end times)
Mk 13:23	So be on your guard; I have told you everything ahead of time.
Mk 13:28	"Now learn this lesson from the fig tree: As soon as its twigs get tender and its leaves come out, you know that summer is near.[...]
Mk 13:29	[...] Even so, when you see these things* happening, you know that it** is near, right at the door. *(#12 Mk 13:4 - Mk 13:21) **(the end)
Mk 13:33	Be on guard! Be alert! You do not know when that time will come.
Mk 13:35	"Therefore keep watch because you do not know when the owner* of the house will come back—whether in the evening, or at midnight, or when the rooster crows, or at dawn. *(the Son of Man)
Mk 13:36	If he* comes suddenly, do not let him find you sleeping. *(the owner of the house - the Son of Man)
Mk 13:37	What I say to you, I say to everyone: 'Watch!'"
Lk 12:36	like servants* waiting for their master to return from a wedding banquet, so that when he comes and knocks they can immediately open the door for him. *(who are dressed with lamps burning) [...]

Lk 12:37	[...] It will be good for those servants whose master finds them watching when he comes. Truly I tell you, he will dress himself to serve, will have them recline at the table and will come and wait on them. [...]
Lk 12:38	[...] It will be good for those servants whose master finds them ready, even if he comes in the middle of the night or toward daybreak.
Lk 12:40	You also* must be ready, because the Son of Man will come at an hour when you do not expect him." *(like vigilant servants)
Lk 12:43	It will be good for that servant whom the master finds doing so* when he returns. *(being faithful)
Lk 12:46	The master of that servant* will come on a day when he does not expect him and at an hour he is not aware of. He will cut him to pieces and assign him a place with the unbelievers. *(who beats others and is drunk) [...]
Lk 12:47	[...] "The servant who knows the master's will and does not get ready or does not do what the master wants will be beaten with many blows. [...]
Lk 12:48	[...] But the one who does not know and does things deserving punishment will be beaten with few blows. From everyone who has been given much, much will be demanded; and from the one who has been entrusted with much, much more will be asked.
Lk 17:23	People will tell you, 'There he is!' or 'Here he is!' Do not go running off after them.

Lk 17:31	On that day* no one who is on the housetop, with possessions inside, should go down to get them. Likewise, no one in the field should go back for anything. *(in end times) [...]
Lk 17:32	[...] Remember Lot's wife!* *(she looked back)
Lk 17:33	Whoever tries to keep their life will lose it, and whoever loses their life will preserve it.
Lk 21:8	He replied: "Watch out that you are not deceived. For many will come in my name, claiming, 'I am he,' and, 'The time is near.' Do not follow them.
Lk 21:9	When you hear of wars and uprisings, do not be frightened. These things must happen first, but the end will not come right away."
Lk 21:14	But make up your mind not to worry beforehand how you will defend yourselves. [...]
Lk 21:15	[...] For I will give you words and wisdom that none of your adversaries will be able to resist or contradict.
Lk 21:20	"When you see Jerusalem being surrounded by armies, you will know that its desolation is near. [...]
Lk 21:21	[...] Then let those who are in Judea flee to the mountains, let those in the city get out, and let those in the country not enter the city.
Lk 21:28	When these things* begin to take place, stand up and lift up your heads, because your redemption is drawing near." *(Lk 21:8 and Lk 21:9)

Lk 21:31	Even so, when you see these things* happening, you know that the kingdom of God is near. *(Lk 21:8, Lk 21:9 & Lk 21:20)
Lk 21:34	"Be careful, or your hearts will be weighed down with carousing, drunkenness and the anxieties of life, and that day will close on you suddenly like a trap. [...]
Lk 21:35	[...] For it will come on all those who live on the face of the whole earth.
Lk 21:36	Be always on the watch, and pray that you may be able to escape all that is about to happen, and that you may be able to stand before the Son of Man."

13. DO <u>ENTER</u> BY THE NARROW GATE

Mt 5:20	For I tell you that unless your righteousness surpasses that of the Pharisees and the teachers of the law, you will certainly not enter the kingdom of heaven.
Mt 7:13	"Enter through the narrow gate. For wide is the gate and broad is the road that leads to destruction, and many enter through it.[...]
Mt 7:14	[...] But small is the gate and narrow the road that leads to life, and only a few find it.
Mt 7:21	"Not everyone who says to me, 'Lord, Lord,' will enter the kingdom of heaven, but only the one who does the will of my Father who is in heaven.
Mt 18:3	And he said: "Truly I tell you, unless you change and become like little children, you will never enter the kingdom of heaven.
Mt 19:17	"Why do you ask me about what is good?" Jesus replied. "There is only One who is good. If you want to enter life, keep the commandments."
Mk 10:15	Truly I tell you, anyone who will not receive the kingdom of God like a little child will never enter it." [Same wording as Lk 18:17]
Lk 13:24	"Make every effort to enter through the narrow door, because many, I tell you, will try to enter and will not be able to.

Lk 18:17	Truly I tell you, anyone who will not receive the kingdom of God like a little child will never enter it." [same wording as Mk 10:15]
Jn 3:5	Jesus answered, "Very truly I tell you, no one can enter the kingdom of God unless they are born of water and the Spirit.
Jn 10:1	"Very truly I tell you Pharisees, anyone who does not enter the sheep pen by the gate, but climbs in by some other way, is a thief and a robber. [...]
Jn 10:2	[...] The one who enters by the gate is the shepherd of the sheep.
Jn 10:7	Therefore Jesus said again, "Very truly I tell you, I am the gate for the sheep.
Jn 10:9	I am the gate; whoever enters through me will be saved. They will come in and go out, and find pasture.
Jn 12:35	Then Jesus told them, "You are going to have the light just a little while longer. Walk while you have the light, before darkness overtakes you. Whoever walks in the dark does not know where they are going.
Jn 14:6	Jesus answered, "I am the way and the truth and the life. No one comes to the Father except through me.

14. DO HAVE FAITH / BELIEVE

Mt 8:10　　When Jesus heard this,* he was amazed and said to those following him, "Truly I tell you, I have not found anyone in Israel with such great faith. *(that a centurion asked that Jesus not come under his roof to heal his servant, rather just say the word) [...]

Mt 8:13　　[...] Then Jesus said to the centurion, "Go! Let it be done just as you believed it would." And his servant was healed at that moment.

Mt 8:26　　He replied, "You* of little faith, why are you so afraid?" Then he got up and rebuked the winds and the waves, and it was completely calm. *(disciples during storm on lake)

Mt 9:2　　Some men brought to him a paralyzed man, lying on a mat. When Jesus saw their faith, he said to the man, "Take heart, son; your sins are forgiven." [...]

Mt 9:6　　[...] But I want you to know that the Son of Man has authority on earth to forgive sins." So he said to the paralyzed man, "Get up, take your mat and go home."

Mt 9:20　　Just then a woman who had been subject to bleeding for twelve years came up behind him and touched the edge of his cloak. [...]

Mt 9:21　　[...] She said to herself, "If I only touch his cloak, I will be healed." [...]

Mt 9:22	[...] Jesus turned and saw her. "Take heart, daughter," he said, "your faith has healed you." And the woman was healed at that moment.
Mt 9:29	Then he touched their* eyes and said, "According to your faith let it be done to you"; *(two blind men)
Mt 13:58	And he did not do many miracles there* because of their lack of faith. *(in his own town)
Mt 14:31	Immediately Jesus reached out his hand and caught him.* "You of little faith," he said, "why did you doubt?"** *(Peter) **(that Peter could walk on water if Jesus was there)
Mt 15:28	Then Jesus said to her,* "Woman, you have great faith! Your request is granted." And her daughter was healed at that moment. *(a Canaanite woman)
Mt 16:8	Aware of their discussion, Jesus asked, "You* of little faith, why are you talking among yourselves about having no bread? *(the disciples) [...]
Mt 16:9	[...] Do you still not understand? Don't you remember the five loaves for the five thousand, and how many basketfuls you gathered?* *(Jesus told them to beware)
Mt 17:20	He replied, "Because you have so little faith. Truly I tell you, if you have faith as small as a mustard seed, you can say to this mountain, 'Move from here to there,' and it will move. Nothing will be impossible for you."

Mt 21:21	Jesus replied,* "Truly I tell you, if you have faith and do not doubt, not only can you do what was done** to the fig tree, but also you can say to this mountain, 'Go, throw yourself into the sea,' and it will be done. *(to the disciples) **(Jesus caused it to wither)
Mt 21:22	If you believe, you will receive whatever you ask for in prayer."
Mt 21:32	For John came to you to show you* the way of righteousness, and you did not believe him, but the tax collectors and the prostitutes did. And even after you saw this, you did not repent and believe him. *(chief priests and elders of the people)
Mt 23:23	"Woe to you, teachers of the law and Pharisees, you hypocrites! You give a tenth of your spices— mint, dill and cumin. But you have neglected the more important matters of the law—justice, mercy and faithfulness. You should have practiced the latter, without neglecting the former.
Mt 24:23	At that time if anyone says to you, 'Look, here is the Messiah!' or, 'There he is!' do not believe it. [...]
Mt 24:26	[...] "So if anyone tells you, 'There he is, out in the wilderness,' do not go out; or, 'Here he is, in the inner rooms,' do not believe it. [...]
Mt 24:27	[...] For as lightning that comes from the east is visible even in the west, so will be the coming of the Son of Man.

Mk 1:15	"The time has come," he said. "The kingdom of God has come near. Repent and believe the good news!"
Mk 2:4	Since they* could not get him** to Jesus because of the crowd, they made an opening in the roof above Jesus by digging through it and then lowered the mat the man was lying on. *(four men carrying a paralytic) **the paralytic) [...]
Mk 2:5	[...] When Jesus saw their* faith, he said to the paralyzed man, "Son, your sins are forgiven." *(four men lowering a paralytic from the roof – Jesus cured the man)
Mk 4:40	He said to his disciples,* "Why are you so afraid? Do you still have no faith?" *(during a storm at sea)
Mk 5:34	He said to her,* "Daughter, your faith has healed you. Go in peace and be freed from your suffering." *(a woman with hemorrhags)
Mk 5:36	Overhearing what they* said,** Jesus told him,*** "Don't be afraid; just believe." *(people from the house of Jairus, the synagogue leader) **("Why bother the teacher anymore?" Since the man's daughter was already dead) ***(Jairus)
Mk 6:6	He was amazed at their* lack of faith. Then Jesus went around teaching from village to village. *(people in his own town)
Mk 9:23	"'If you can'?" said Jesus,* "Everything is possible for one who believes." *(to a father of a son with a mute spirit who said, "If you can do anything have compassion on us.") [...]

67

Mk 9:24	[...] Immediately the boy's father exclaimed, "I do believe; help me overcome my unbelief!"
Mk 10:15	Truly I tell you, anyone who will not receive the kingdom of God like a little child will never enter it." [Same wording as Lk 18:17]
Mk 10:52	"Go," said Jesus, "your* faith has healed you." Immediately he received his sight and followed Jesus along the road. *(blind Bartimaeus)
Mk 11:22	"Have faith in God," Jesus answered.* *(the disciples) [...]
Mk 11:23	[...] "Truly I tell you, if anyone says to this mountain, 'Go, throw yourself into the sea,' and does not doubt in their heart but believes that what they say will happen, it will be done for them.
Mk 11:24	Therefore I tell you, whatever you ask for in prayer, believe that you have received it, and it will be yours.
Mk 13:21	At that time* if anyone says to you, 'Look, here is the Messiah!' or, 'Look, there he is!' do not believe it. *(end times)
Mk 14:27	"You will all fall away," Jesus told them,* "for it is written: " 'I will strike the shepherd, and the sheep will be scattered.' *(the disciples) [...]
Mk 14:29	[...] Peter declared, "Even if all fall away, I will not."* *(but he was shaken)
Mk 16:14	Later Jesus appeared to the Eleven as they were eating; he rebuked them for their lack of faith and their stubborn refusal to believe those who had seen him after he had risen.

Mk 16:16   Whoever believes and is baptized will be saved, but whoever does not believe will be condemned.

Lk 5:20   When Jesus saw their* faith, he said, "Friend, your sins are forgiven."** *(four men lowering a paralytic from the roof) **(and he healed him)

Lk 7:9   When Jesus heard this,* he was amazed at him, and turning to the crowd following him, he said, "I tell you, I have not found such great faith even in Israel." *(that a centurion who had a sick servant and told Jesus not to come to his house rather just say the word) [...]

Lk 7:10   [...] Then the men who had been sent returned to the house and found the servant well.

Lk 7:50   Jesus said to the woman,* "Your faith has saved you; go in peace." *(the sinful woman who kissed his feet)

Lk 8:25   "Where is your faith?" he asked his disciples.* In fear and amazement they asked one another, "Who is this? He commands even the winds and the water, and they obey him." *(during a storm at sea)

Lk 8:48   Then he said to her,* "Daughter, your faith has healed you. Go in peace." *(a woman subject to bleeding for twelve years)

Lk 8:49   While Jesus was still speaking, someone came from the house of Jairus, the synagogue leader. "Your daughter is dead," he said. "Don't bother the teacher anymore." [...]

Lk 8:50	[...] Hearing this,* Jesus said to Jairus, "Don't be afraid; just believe, and she will be healed." *(Lk 8:49)
Lk 12:28	If that is how God clothes the grass of the field, which is here today, and tomorrow is thrown into the fire, how much more will he clothe you—you of little faith!
Lk 17:6	He replied, "If you have faith as small as a mustard seed, you can say to this mulberry tree, 'Be uprooted and planted in the sea,' and it will obey you.
Lk 17:19	Then he said to him,* "Rise and go; your faith has made you well." *(a Samaritan leper who was cured)
Lk 18:17	Truly I tell you, anyone who will not receive the kingdom of God like a little child will never enter it." [same wording as Mk 10:15]
Lk 18:42	Jesus said to him,* "Receive your sight; your faith has healed you." *(a blind man)
Lk 22:32	But I have prayed for you, Simon, that your faith may not fail. And when you have turned back, strengthen your brothers."
Jn 1:12	Yet to all who did receive him, to those who believed in his name, he gave the right to become children of God -
Jn 1:50	Jesus said, "You believe because I told you I saw you under the fig tree. You will see greater things than that."

Jn 2:11   What Jesus did* here in Cana of Galilee was the first of the signs through which he revealed his glory; and his disciples believed in him. *(changing water into wine)

Jn 2:22   After he was raised from the dead, his disciples recalled what he had said.* Then they believed the scripture and the words that Jesus had spoken. *("Destroy this temple and in three days I will raise it up.")

Jn 2:23   Now while he was in Jerusalem at the Passover Festival, many people saw the signs he was performing and believed in his name.

Jn 3:15   that everyone who believes may have eternal life in him."

Jn 3:16   For God so loved the world that he gave his one and only Son, that whoever believes in him shall not perish but have eternal life.

Jn 3:18   Whoever believes in him is not condemned, but whoever does not believe stands condemned already because they have not believed in the name of God's one and only Son.

Jn 3:36   Whoever believes in the Son has eternal life, but whoever rejects the Son will not see life, for God's wrath remains on them.

Jn 4:21   "Woman," Jesus replied, "believe me, a time is coming when you will worship the Father neither on this mountain nor in Jerusalem.

Jn 4:39   Many of the Samaritans from that town believed in him because of the woman's testimony, "He told me everything I ever did." [...]

Jn 4:41	[...] And because of his words many more became believers. [...]
Jn 4:42	[...] They said to the woman, "We no longer believe just because of what you said; now we have heard for ourselves, and we know that this man really is the Savior of the world."
Jn 4:53	Then the father realized that this was the exact time at which Jesus had said to him, "Your son will live." So he and his whole household believed.
Jn 5:24	"Very truly I tell you, whoever hears my word and believes him who sent me has eternal life and will not be judged but has crossed over from death to life.
Jn 5:46	If you believed Moses, you would believe me, for he wrote about me.
Jn 6:29	Jesus answered,* "The work of God is this: to believe in the one he has sent." *(the crowd)
Jn 6:35	Then Jesus declared, "I am the bread of life. Whoever comes to me will never go hungry, and whoever believes in me will never be thirsty.
Jn 6:40	For my Father's will is that everyone who looks to the Son and believes in him shall have eternal life, and I will raise them up at the last day."
Jn 6:47	Very truly I tell you, the one who believes has eternal life.
Jn 6:68	Simon Peter answered him, "Lord, to whom shall we go? You have the words of eternal life. [...]

Jn 6:69	[...] We* have come to believe and to know that you are the Holy One of God." *(Peter and the eleven)
Jn 7:31	Still, many in the crowd believed in him. They said, "When the Messiah comes, will he perform more signs than this man?"
Jn 7:38	Whoever believes in me, as Scripture has said, rivers of living water will flow from within them."
Jn 8:24	I told you that you would die in your sins; if you do not believe that I am he, you will indeed die in your sins." [...]
Jn 8:30	[...] Even as he spoke, many believed in him.
Jn 8:31	To the Jews who had believed him, Jesus said, "If you hold to my teaching, you are really my disciples. [...]
Jn 8:32	[...] Then you will know the truth, and the truth will set you free."
Jn 8:46	Can any of you prove me guilty of sin? If I am telling the truth, why don't you believe me?
Jn 9:38	Then the man* said, "Lord, I believe," and he worshiped him. *(born blind and cured)
Jn 10:37	Do not believe me unless I do the works of my Father. [...]
Jn 10:38	[...] But if I do them, even though you do not believe me, believe the works, that you may know and understand that the Father is in me, and I in the Father."
Jn 10:42	And in that place* many believed in Jesus. *(across the Jordan)

Jn 11:15	and for your sake I am glad I was not there,* so that you may believe. But let us go to him."** *(when Lazarus died) **(Lazarus)
Jn 11:25	Jesus said to her,* "I am the resurrection and the life. The one who believes in me will live, even though they die; *(Martha) [...]
Jn 11:26	[...] and whoever lives by believing in me will never die. Do you believe this?" [...]
Jn 11:27	[...] "Yes, Lord," she replied, "I believe that you are the Messiah, the Son of God, who is to come into the world."
Jn 11:40	Then Jesus said,* "Did I not tell you that if you believe, you will see the glory of God?" *(to Martha)
Jn 11:42	I knew that you* always hear me, but I said this for the benefit of the people standing here,** that they may believe that you sent me." *(God) **(by Lazarus tomb)
Jn 11:45	Therefore many of the Jews who had come to visit Mary, and had seen what Jesus did,* believed in him. *(raising Lazarus from the dead)
Jn 12:11	for on account of him* many of the Jews were going over to Jesus and believing in him. *(Lazarus)
Jn 12:35	Then Jesus told them, "You are going to have the light just a little while longer. Walk while you have the light, before darkness overtakes you. Whoever walks in the dark does not know where they are going. [...]

Jn 12:36	[...] Believe in the light while you have the light, so that you may become children of light." When he had finished speaking, Jesus left and hid himself from them.* *(the crowd)
Jn 12:42	Yet at the same time many even among the leaders believed in him. But because of the Pharisees they would not openly acknowledge their faith for fear they would be put out of the synagogue;
Jn 12:44	Then Jesus cried out, "Whoever believes in me does not believe in me only, but in the one who sent me.
Jn 12:46	I have come into the world as a light, so that no one who believes in me should stay in darkness.
Jn 13:20	Very truly I tell you, whoever accepts anyone I send accepts me; and whoever accepts me accepts the one who sent me."
Jn 14:1	"Do not let your hearts be troubled. You believe in God; believe also in me.
Jn 14:11	Believe me when I say that I am in the Father and the Father is in me; or at least believe on the evidence of the works themselves.
Jn 14:12	Very truly I tell you, whoever believes in me will do the works I have been doing, and they will do even greater things than these, because I am going to the Father.
Jn 14:28	"You heard me say, 'I am going away and I am coming back to you.' If you loved me, you would be glad that I am going to the Father, for the Father is greater than I. [...]

Jn 14:29	[...] I have told you now before it* happens, so that when it does happen you will believe. *(Jn 14:28)
Jn 16:8	When he* comes, he will prove the world to be in the wrong about sin and righteousness and judgment: *(the Advocate) [...]
Jn 16:9	[...] about sin, because people do not believe in me;
Jn 16:27	No, the Father himself loves you because you have loved me and have believed that I came from God.
Jn 16:30	Now we* can see that you* know all things and that you do not even need to have anyone ask you questions. This makes us believe that you came from God." *(the disciples) **(Jesus)
Jn 17:3	Now this is eternal life: that they* know you, the only true God, and Jesus Christ, whom you have sent. *(all people given to Jesus)
Jn 17:8	For I gave them* the words you** gave me and they accepted them. They knew with certainty that I came from you, and they believed that you sent me. *(those in the world given by God to Jesus) **(God)
Jn 17:20	"My prayer is not for them* alone. I pray also for those who will believe in me through their message, *(those in the world given by God to Jesus) [...]

Jn 17:21   [...] that all of them* may be one, Father, just as you are in me and I am in you. May they also be in us so that the world may believe that you have sent me. *(those in the world given by God to Jesus)

Jn 19:35   The man who saw it* has given testimony, and his testimony is true. He knows that he tells the truth, and he testifies so that you also may believe. *(that blood and water came from Jesus side after his death)

Jn 20:27   Then he said to Thomas, "Put your finger here; see my hands. Reach out your hand and put it into my side. Stop doubting and believe."

Jn 20:29   Then Jesus told him,* "Because you have seen me, you have believed; blessed are those who have not seen and yet have believed." *(Thomas)

Jn 20:31   But these* are written that you may believe that Jesus is the Messiah, the Son of God, and that by believing you may have life in his name. *(signs)

15. DO <u>FOLLOW</u> / COME

Mt 4:18	As Jesus was walking beside the Sea of Galilee, he saw two brothers, Simon called Peter and his brother Andrew. They were casting a net into the lake, for they were fishermen. [...]
Mt 4:19	[...] "Come, follow me," Jesus said, "and I will send you out to fish for people."
Mt 4:21	Going on from there, he saw two other brothers, James son of Zebedee and his brother John. They were in a boat with their father Zebedee, preparing their nets. Jesus called them, [...]
Mt 4:22	[...] and immediately they* left the boat and their father and followed him. *(James and John)
Mt 4:25	Large crowds from Galilee, the Decapolis, Jerusalem, Judea and the region across the Jordan followed him.* *(Jesus)
Mt 8:22	But Jesus told him,* "Follow me, and let the dead bury their own dead." *(a disciple)
Mt 9:9	As Jesus went on from there, he saw a man named Matthew sitting at the tax collector's booth. "Follow me," he told him, and Matthew got up and followed him.
Mt 10:38	Whoever does not take up their cross and follow me is not worthy of me.
Mt 11:28	"Come to me,* all you who are weary and burdened, and I will give you rest. *(Jesus)

Mt 11:29	Take my yoke upon you and learn from me,* for I am gentle and humble in heart, and you will find rest for your souls. *(Jesus)
Mt 14:28	"Lord, if it's you," Peter replied, "tell me to come to you on the water." [...]
Mt 14:29	[...] "Come," he* said. Then Peter got down out of the boat, walked on the water and came toward Jesus. *(Jesus)
Mt 16:24	Then Jesus said to his disciples, "Whoever wants to be my disciple must deny themselves and take up their cross and follow me.
Mt 19:14	Jesus said, "Let the little children come to me, and do not hinder them, for the kingdom of heaven belongs to such as these."
Mt 19:21	Jesus answered,* "If you want to be perfect, go, sell your possessions and give to the poor, and you will have treasure in heaven. Then come, follow me." *(a wealthy man with many possessions who had kept all God's commandments)
Mt 28:10	Then Jesus said to them,* "Do not be afraid. Go and tell my brothers to go to Galilee; there they will see me." *(Mary Magdalene and the other Mary)
Mk 1:16	As Jesus walked beside the Sea of Galilee, he saw Simon and his brother Andrew casting a net into the lake, for they were fishermen.[...]
Mk 1:17	[...] "Come, follow me," Jesus said,* "and I will send you out to fish for people." *(to Simon and Andrew)

Mk 1:19	When he had gone a little farther, he saw James son of Zebedee and his brother John in a boat, preparing their nets. [...]
Mk 1:20	[...] Without delay he called them,* and they left their father Zebedee in the boat with the hired men and followed him. *(James and John)
Mk 2:14	As he walked along, he saw Levi son of Alphaeus sitting at the tax collector's booth. "Follow me," Jesus told him, and Levi got up and followed him.
Mk 6:31	Then, because so many people were coming and going that they* did not even have a chance to eat, he said to them, "Come with me by yourselves to a quiet place and get some rest." *(the apostles)
Mk 8:34	Then he called the crowd to him along with his disciples and said: "Whoever wants to be my disciple must deny themselves and take up their cross and follow me.
Mk 10:13	People were bringing little children to Jesus for him to place his hands on them, but the disciples rebuked them. [...]
Mk 10:14	[...] When Jesus saw this,* he was indignant. He said to them, "Let the little children come to me, and do not hinder them, for the kingdom of God belongs to such as these. *(Mk 10:13)

Mk 10:21	Jesus looked at him* and loved him. "One thing you lack," he said. "Go, sell everything you have and give to the poor, and you will have treasure in heaven. Then come, follow me." *(a wealthy man who had kept all of God's commandments who wanted to know how to inherit eternal life)
Mk 10:52	"Go," said Jesus, "your* faith has healed you." Immediately he received his sight and followed Jesus along the road. *(blind Bartimaeus)
Lk 5:11	So they* pulled their boats up on shore, left everything and followed him. *(Simon Peter, James and John)
Lk 5:27	After this, Jesus went out and saw a tax collector by the name of Levi sitting at his tax booth. "Follow me,"* Jesus said to him, *(he followed)
Lk 9:11	but the crowds learned about it* and followed him. He welcomed them and spoke to them about the kingdom of God, and healed those who needed healing. *(that Jesus and the apostles had withdrawn to Bethsaida)
Lk 9:23	Then he said to them all: "Whoever wants to be my disciple must deny themselves and take up their cross daily and follow me.
Lk 9:59	He said to another man, "Follow me." But he replied, "Lord, first let me go and bury my father." [...]
Lk 9:60	[...] Jesus said to him, "Let the dead bury their own dead, but you go and proclaim the kingdom of God."

Lk 9:61	Still another said, "I will follow you, Lord; but first let me go back and say goodbye to my family." [...]
Lk 9:62	[...] Jesus replied, "No one who puts a hand to the plow and looks back is fit for service in the kingdom of God."
Lk 14:26	"If anyone comes to me and does not hate father and mother, wife and children, brothers and sisters—yes, even their own life—such a person cannot be my disciple.
Lk 14:27	And whoever does not carry their cross and follow me cannot be my disciple.
Lk 18:16	But Jesus called the children to him and said, "Let the little children come to me, and do not hinder them, for the kingdom of God belongs to such as these.
Lk 18:22	When Jesus heard this,* he said to him,** "You still lack one thing. Sell everything you have and give to the poor, and you will have treasure in heaven. Then come, follow me." *(the question of how one should inherit eternal life if he has obeyed all the commandments since his youth) **(a wealthy ruler)
Lk 18:43	Immediately he* received his sight and followed Jesus, praising God. When all the people saw it, they also praised God. *(a blind man)
Jn 1:37	When the two disciples* heard him** say this,*** they followed Jesus. *(Andrew and another) **(John) ***("Look the Lamb of God.")

Jn 1:39	"Come," he replied, "and you will see."* So they went and saw where he was staying, and they spent that day with him. It was about four in the afternoon. (to the two disciples of John who inquired where was Jesus staying)
Jn 1:43	The next day Jesus decided to leave for Galilee. Finding Philip, he said to him, "Follow me."
Jn 6:35	Then Jesus declared, "I am the bread of life. Whoever comes to me will never go hungry, and whoever believes in me will never be thirsty.
Jn 6:65	He went on to say, "This is why I told you that no one can come to me unless the Father has enabled them."
Jn 7:37	On the last and greatest day of the festival, Jesus stood and said in a loud voice, "Let anyone who is thirsty come to me and drink.
Jn 8:12	When Jesus spoke again to the people, he said, "I am the light of the world. Whoever follows me will never walk in darkness, but will have the light of life."
Jn 10:27	My sheep listen to my voice; I know them, and they follow me.
Jn 12:26	Whoever serves me must follow me; and where I am, my servant also will be. My Father will honor the one who serves me.
Jn 13:15	I have set you an example that you should do as I have done for you.
Jn 13:36	Simon Peter asked him, "Lord, where are you going?" Jesus replied, "Where I am going, you cannot follow now, but you will follow later."

Jn 15:8	This is to my Father's glory, that you bear much fruit, showing yourselves to be my disciples.
Jn 21:18	Very truly I tell you, when you were younger you dressed yourself and went where you wanted; but when you are old you will stretch out your hands, and someone else will dress you and lead you where you do not want to go." [...]
Jn 21:19	[...] Jesus said this to indicate the kind of death by which Peter would glorify God. Then he said to him, "Follow me!"
Jn 21:22	Jesus answered,* "If I want him** to remain alive until I return, what is that to you? You must follow me." *(Peter) **(the disciple Jesus loved)

16. DO FORGIVE / SHOW MERCY

Mt 5:7	Blessed are the merciful, for they will be shown mercy.
Mt 6:12	And forgive us our debts, as we also have forgiven our debtors.
Mt 6:14	For if you forgive other people when they sin against you, your heavenly Father will also forgive you.
Mt 6:15	But if you do not forgive others their sins, your Father will not forgive your sins.
Mt 9:2	Some men brought to him a paralyzed man, lying on a mat. When Jesus saw their faith, he said to the man, "Take heart, son; your sins are forgiven." [...]
Mt 9:6	[...] But I want you to know that the Son of Man has authority on earth to forgive sins." So he said to the paralyzed man, "Get up, take your mat and go home."
Mt 9:13	But go and learn what this means: 'I desire mercy, not sacrifice.' For I have not come to call the righteous, but sinners."
Mt 12:7	If you had known what these words mean, 'I desire mercy, not sacrifice,' you would not have condemned the innocent.
Mt 12:31	And so I tell you, every kind of sin and slander can be forgiven, but blasphemy against the Spirit will not be forgiven.

Mt 12:32	Anyone who speaks a word against the Son of Man will be forgiven, but anyone who speaks against the Holy Spirit will not be forgiven, either in this age or in the age to come.
Mt 16:19	I will give you* the keys of the kingdom of heaven; whatever you bind on earth will be bound in heaven, and whatever you loose on earth will be loosed in heaven." *(Peter)
Mt 18:18	"Truly I tell you, whatever you bind on earth will be bound in heaven, and whatever you loose on earth will be loosed in heaven.
Mt 18:21	Then Peter came to Jesus and asked, "Lord, how many times shall I forgive my brother or sister who sins against me? Up to seven times?" [...]
Mt 18:22	[...] Jesus answered, "I tell you, not seven times, but seventy-seven times.
Mt 18:34	In anger his master handed him* over to the jailers to be tortured, until he should pay back all he owed. *(the unforgiving servant) [...]
Mt 18:35	[...] "This is how my heavenly Father will treat each of you unless you forgive your brother or sister from your heart."
Mt 23:23	"Woe to you, teachers of the law and Pharisees, you hypocrites! You give a tenth of your spices—mint, dill and cumin. But you have neglected the more important matters of the law—justice, mercy and faithfulness. You should have practiced the latter, without neglecting the former.

Mk 2:5	When Jesus saw their* faith, he said to the paralyzed man, "Son, your sins are forgiven." *(four men lowering a paralytic from the roof) [...]
Mk 2:10	[...] But I want you to know that the Son of Man has authority on earth to forgive sins." So he said to the man, [...]
Mk 2:11	[...] "I tell you, get up, take your mat and go home."
Mk 3:28	Truly I tell you, people can be forgiven all their sins and every slander they utter, [...]
Mk 3:29	[...] but whoever blasphemes against the Holy Spirit will never be forgiven; they are guilty of an eternal sin."
Mk 5:19	Jesus did not let him,* but said, "Go home to your own people and tell them how much the Lord has done for you, and how he has had mercy on you." *(a demon possessed man who Jesus cured)
Mk 11:25	And when you stand praying, if you hold anything against anyone, forgive them, so that your Father in heaven may forgive you your sins."
Lk 1:50	His* mercy extends to those who fear him, from generation to generation. *(God)
Lk 1:54	He* has helped his servant Israel, remembering to be merciful *(God)
Lk 1:57	When it was time for Elizabeth to have her baby, she gave birth to a son.* *(John the Baptist) [...]

Lk 1:58	[...] Her neighbors and relatives heard that the Lord had shown her great mercy, and they shared her joy.
Lk 1:72	to show mercy to our ancestors and to remember his* holy covenant,** *(God) **(part of the song of Zechariah, father of John the Baptist)
Lk 1:78	Because* of the tender mercy of our God, by which the rising sun will come to us from heaven *(part of the song of Zechariah, father of John the Baptist)
Lk 5:20	When Jesus saw their* faith, he said, "Friend, your sins are forgiven." *(four men lowering a paralytic from the roof) [...]
Lk 5:24	[...] But I want you to know that the Son of Man has authority on earth to forgive sins." So he said to the paralyzed man, "I tell you, get up, take your mat and go home."
Lk 6:36	Be merciful, just as your Father is merciful.
Lk 6:37	"Do not judge, and you will not be judged. Do not condemn, and you will not be condemned. Forgive, and you will be forgiven.
Lk 7:47	Therefore, I tell you, her* many sins have been forgiven—as her great love has shown. But whoever has been forgiven little loves little." *(a woman who kissed and wiped Jesus' feet) [...]
Lk 7:48	[...] Then Jesus said to her, "Your sins are forgiven."

Lk 10:36	"Which of these three* do you think was a neighbor to the man who fell into the hands of robbers?" *(two unhelpful walkers and one helpful walker) [...]
Lk 10:37	[...] The expert in the law replied, "The one who had mercy on him." Jesus told him, "Go and do likewise."
Lk 11:4	Forgive us our sins, for we also forgive everyone who sins against us. And lead us not into temptation.'"
Lk 12:10	And everyone who speaks a word against the Son of Man will be forgiven, but anyone who blasphemes against the Holy Spirit will not be forgiven.
Lk 17:3	So watch yourselves. "If your brother or sister sins against you, rebuke them; and if they repent, forgive them.
Lk 17:4	Even if they* sin against you seven times in a day and seven times come back to you saying 'I repent,' you must forgive them." *(your brother or sister)
Lk 18:10	"Two men went up to the temple to pray, one a Pharisee and the other a tax collector. [...]
Lk 18:14	[...] "I tell you that this man,* rather than the other,** went home justified before God. For all those who exalt themselves will be humbled, and those who humble themselves will be exalted." *(a humble tax collector who asked for mercy) **(a proud Pharisee who praised himself)

Lk 19:10	For the Son of Man came to seek and to save the lost."
Lk 23:34	Jesus said,* "Father, forgive them,** for they do not know what they are doing." And they divided up his clothes by casting lots. *(while on the cross) **(his persecutors)
Jn 20:23	If you* forgive anyone's sins, their sins are forgiven; if you do not forgive them, they are not forgiven." *(the disciples)

17. DO <u>GOOD DEEDS</u> / BE RIGHTEOUS

Mt 3:15   Jesus replied, "Let it* be so now; it is proper for us to do this to fulfill all righteousness." Then John consented. *(to baptize Jesus)

Mt 5:6   Blessed are those who hunger and thirst for righteousness, for they will be filled.

Mt 5:10   Blessed are those who are persecuted because of righteousness, for theirs is the kingdom of heaven.

Mt 5:16   In the same way,* let your light shine before others, that they may see your good deeds and glorify your Father in heaven. *(as you would put a lamp on a stand to light the house)

Mt 5:20   For I tell you that unless your righteousness surpasses that of the Pharisees and the teachers of the law, you will certainly not enter the kingdom of heaven.

Mt 6:1   "Be careful not to practice your righteousness in front of others to be seen by them. If you do, you will have no reward from your Father in heaven.

Mt 6:20   But store up for yourselves treasures in heaven, where moths and vermin do not destroy, and where thieves do not break in and steal.

Mt 6:33   But seek first his kingdom and his righteousness, and all these things will be given to you as well.

Mt 10:41	Whoever welcomes a prophet as a prophet will receive a prophet's reward, and whoever welcomes a righteous person as a righteous person will receive a righteous person's reward.
Mt 11:21	"Woe to you, Chorazin! Woe to you, Bethsaida! For if the miracles that were performed in you had been performed in Tyre and Sidon, they would have repented long ago in sackcloth and ashes.
Mt 11:23	And you, Capernaum, will you be lifted to the heavens? No, you will go down to Hades. For if the miracles that were performed in you had been performed in Sodom, it would have remained to this day.
Mt 13:43	Then* the righteous will shine like the sun in the kingdom of their Father. Whoever has ears, let them hear. *(at the end of the age after the sinful are gone)
Mt 21:32	For John came to you to show you* the way of righteousness, and you did not believe him, but the tax collectors and the prostitutes did. And even after you saw this, you did not repent and believe him. *(chief priests and elders of the people)
Mt 23:28	In the same way, on the outside you* appear to people as righteous but on the inside you are full of hypocrisy and wickedness. *(teachers of the law and Pharisees)

Mt 25:40	"The King* will reply,** 'Truly I tell you,** whatever you did for one of the least of these brothers and sisters of mine, you did for me.' *(the Son of Man) **(to the righteous on his right) [...]
Mt 25:45	[...] "He* will reply, 'Truly I tell you, **whatever you did not do for one of the least of these, you did not do for me.' *(the King - the Son of Man) **(to the accursed on his left) [...]
Mt 25:46	[...] "Then they* will go away to eternal punishment, but the righteous** to eternal life." *(Mt 25:45) **(Mt 25:40)
Lk 1:74	to rescue us* from the hand of our enemies, and to enable us to serve him without fear *(prophesy of Zechariah, father of John the Baptist) [...]
Lk 1:75	[...] in holiness and righteousness before him all our days.
Lk 6:27	"But to you who are listening I say: Love your enemies, do good to those who hate you,
Lk 6:28	bless those who curse you, pray for those who mistreat you.
Lk 6:29	If someone slaps you on one cheek, turn to them the other also. If someone takes your coat, do not withhold your shirt from them.
Lk 6:30	Give to everyone who asks you, and if anyone takes what belongs to you, do not demand it back.
Lk 6:31	Do to others as you would have them do to you.

Lk 6:35	But love your enemies, do good to them, and lend to them without expecting to get anything back. Then your reward will be great, and you will be children of the Most High, because he is kind to the ungrateful and wicked.
Lk 6:45	A good man brings good things out of the good stored up in his heart, and an evil man brings evil things out of the evil stored up in his heart. For the mouth speaks what the heart is full of.
Lk 10:36	"Which of these three* do you think was a neighbor to the man who fell into the hands of robbers?" *(two unhelpful walkers and one helpful walker) [...]
Lk 10:37	[...]The expert in the law replied, "The one who had mercy on him." Jesus told him, "Go and do likewise."
Lk 19:37	When he came near the place where the road goes down the Mount of Olives, the whole crowd of disciples began joyfully to praise God in loud voices for all the miracles* they had seen: *(deeds)
Jn 3:21	But whoever lives by the truth comes into the light, so that it may be seen plainly that what they have done has been done in the sight of God.
Jn 5:28	"Do not be amazed at this, for a time is coming when all who are in their graves will hear his voice [...]
Jn 5:29	[...] and come out—those who have done what is good will rise to live, and those who have done what is evil will rise to be condemned.

Jn 16:8   When he* comes, he will prove the world to be in the wrong about sin and righteousness and judgment: *(the Advocate) [...]

Jn 16:10   [...] about righteousness, because I am going to the Father, where you can see me no longer;

18. DO BE <u>HUMBLE</u> / MEEK

Mt 5:5	Blessed are the meek, for they will inherit the earth.
Mt 11:29	Take my yoke upon you and learn from me,* for I am gentle and humble in heart, and you will find rest for your souls. *(Jesus)
Mt 18:3	And he said: "Truly I tell you, unless you change and become like little children, you will never enter the kingdom of heaven.
Mt 18:4	Therefore, whoever takes the lowly position of this child is the greatest in the kingdom of heaven.
Mt 19:14	Jesus said, "Let the little children come to me, and do not hinder them, for the kingdom of heaven belongs to such as these."
Mt 23:12	For those who exalt themselves will be humbled, and those who humble themselves will be exalted.
Mk 7:21	For it is from within, out of a person's heart, that evil thoughts come—sexual immorality, theft, murder, [...]
Mk 7:22	[...] adultery, greed, malice, deceit, lewdness, envy, slander, arrogance and folly. [...]
Mk 7:23	[...] All these* evils come from inside and defile a person." *(Mk 7:21 and Mk 7:22)
Mk 10:13	People were bringing little children to Jesus for him to place his hands on them, but the disciples rebuked them. [...]

Mk 10:14	[...] When Jesus saw this,* he was indignant. He said to them, "Let the little children come to me, and do not hinder them, for the kingdom of God belongs to such as these. *(Mk 10:13)
Mk 10:15	Truly I tell you, anyone who will not receive the kingdom of God like a little child will never enter it." [Same wording as Lk 18:17]
Lk 1:48	for he* has been mindful of the humble state of his servant. From now on all generations will call me** blessed, *(God) **(Mary)
Lk 1:52	He* has brought down rulers from their thrones but has lifted up the humble. *(God)
Lk 9:48	Then he said to them,* "Whoever welcomes this little child in my name welcomes me; and whoever welcomes me welcomes the one who sent me. For it is the one who is least among you all who is the greatest." *(the disciples)
Lk 14:11	For all those who exalt themselves will be humbled, and those who humble themselves will be exalted."
Lk 18:10	"Two men went up to the temple to pray, one a Pharisee and the other a tax collector. [...]
Lk 18:14	[...] "I tell you that this man,* rather than the other,** went home justified before God. For all those who exalt themselves will be humbled, and those who humble themselves will be exalted." *(a humble tax collector who asked for mercy) **(a proud Pharisee who praised himself)

Lk 18:16 But Jesus called the children to him and said, "Let the little children come to me, and do not hinder them, for the kingdom of God belongs to such as these.

Lk 18:17 Truly I tell you, anyone who will not receive the kingdom of God like a little child will never enter it." [same wording as Mk 10:15]

19. DON'T JUDGE / CONDEMN

Mt 7:1   "Do not judge, or you too will be judged.

Mt 7:2   For in the same way you judge others, you will be judged, and with the measure you use, it will be measured to you.

Lk 6:37   "Do not judge, and you will not be judged. Do not condemn, and you will not be condemned. Forgive, and you will be forgiven.

Jn 5:22   Moreover, the Father judges no one, but has entrusted all judgment to the Son,

Jn 5:27   And he* has given him** authority to judge because he is the Son of Man. *(God) **(Jesus)

Jn 7:24   Stop judging by mere appearances, but instead judge correctly."

Jn 8:7   When they* kept on questioning him, he straightened up and said to them, "Let any one of you who is without sin be the first to throw a stone at her."** *(the teachers of the law and the Pharisees) **(a woman caught in the act of adultery) [...]

Jn 8:10   [...] Jesus straightened up and asked her, "Woman, where are they? Has no one condemned you?" [...]

Jn 8:11   [...] "No one, sir," she* said. "Then neither do I condemn you," Jesus declared. "Go now and leave your life of sin." *(a woman caught in the act of adultery)

Jn 8:15	You judge by human standards; I pass judgment on no one.
Jn 8:16	But if I do judge, my decisions are true, because I am not alone. I stand with the Father, who sent me.
Jn 12:47	"If anyone hears my words but does not keep them, I do not judge that person. For I did not come to judge the world, but to save the world.
Jn 12:48	There is a judge for the one who rejects me and does not accept my words; the very words I have spoken will condemn them at the last day.

20. DO HAVE RIGHT JUDGEMENT

Mt 23:23   "Woe to you, teachers of the law and Pharisees, you hypocrites! You give a tenth of your spices—mint, dill and cumin. But you have neglected the more important matters of the law—justice, mercy and faithfulness. You should have practiced the latter, without neglecting the former.

Lk 11:42   "Woe to you Pharisees, because you give God a tenth of your mint, rue and all other kinds of garden herbs, but you neglect justice and the love of God. You should have practiced the latter without leaving the former undone.

Jn 5:30   By myself I can do nothing; I judge only as I hear, and my judgment is just, for I seek not to please myself but him who sent me.

Jn 8:15   You judge by human standards; I pass judgment on no one.

Jn 16:8   When he* comes, he will prove the world to be in the wrong about sin and righteousness and judgment: *(the Advocate) [...]

Jn 16:11   [...] and about judgment, because the prince of this world now stands condemned.

21. DO <u>KEEP THE COMMANDMENTS</u>

Mt 4:4   Jesus answered,* "It is written: 'Man shall not live on bread alone, but on every word that comes from the mouth of God.'" *(to the devil)

Mt 5:19   Therefore anyone who sets aside one of the least of these commands and teaches others accordingly will be called least in the kingdom of heaven, but whoever practices and teaches these commands will be called great in the kingdom of heaven.

Mt 19:17   "Why do you ask me about what is good?" Jesus replied. "There is only One who is good. If you want to enter life, keep the commandments."

Mt 23:23   "Woe to you, teachers of the law and Pharisees, you hypocrites! You give a tenth of your spices—mint, dill and cumin. But you have neglected the more important matters of the law—justice, mercy and faithfulness. You should have practiced the latter, without neglecting the former.

Mt 28:20   and teaching them* to obey everything I have commanded you. And surely I am with you always, to the very end of the age." *(disciples of all nations)

Mk 7:8   You* have let go of the commands of God and are holding on to human traditions." *(Pharisees and teachers of the law)

Mk 10:19	You know the commandments: 'You shall not murder, you shall not commit adultery, you shall not steal, you shall not give false testimony, you shall not defraud, honor your father and mother.'"
Lk 4:4	Jesus answered,* "It is written: 'Man shall not live on bread alone.'" *(to the devil) [see Mt 4:4]
Lk 6:46	"Why do you call me, 'Lord, Lord,' and do not do what I say?
Lk 11:28	He replied,* "Blessed rather are those who hear the word of God and obey it." *(to a woman in the crowd)
Lk 17:10	So you also, when you have done everything you were told to do, should say, 'We are unworthy servants; we have only done our duty.'"
Lk 18:20	You know the commandments: 'You shall not commit adultery, you shall not murder, you shall not steal, you shall not give false testimony, honor your father and mother.'"
Jn 8:31	To the Jews who had believed him, Jesus said, "If you hold to my teaching, you are really my disciples. [...]
Jn 8:32	[...] Then you will know the truth, and the truth will set you free."
Jn 8:51	Very truly I tell you, whoever obeys my word will never see death."
Jn 8:55	Though you do not know him,* I know him. If I said I did not, I would be a liar like you, but I do know him and obey his word. *(God)

Jn 12:48	There is a judge for the one who rejects me and does not accept my words; the very words I have spoken will condemn them at the last day.
Jn 12:50	I know that his command leads to eternal life. So whatever I say is just what the Father has told me to say."
Jn 14:15	"If you love me, keep my commands.
Jn 14:21	Whoever has my commands and keeps them is the one who loves me. The one who loves me will be loved by my Father, and I too will love them and show myself to them."
Jn 14:23	Jesus replied,* "Anyone who loves me will obey my teaching. My Father will love them, and we will come to them and make our home with them. *(to Judas not Judas Iscariot)
Jn 14:31	but he* comes so that the world may learn that I love the Father and do exactly what my Father has commanded me. "Come now; let us leave. *(the prince of this world)
Jn 15:10	If you keep my commands, you will remain in my love, just as I have kept my Father's commands and remain in his love.
Jn 15:14	You are my friends if you do what I command.
Jn 17:6	"I have revealed you* to those whom you gave me out of the world. They were yours; you gave them to me and they have obeyed your word. *(God)

22. DO LEARN

Mt 6:28 "And why do you worry about clothes? See* how the flowers of the field grow. They do not labor or spin. *(learn)

Mt 9:13 But go and learn what this means: 'I desire mercy, not sacrifice.' For I have not come to call the righteous, but sinners."

Mt 11:29 Take my yoke upon you and learn from me,* for I am gentle and humble in heart, and you will find rest for your souls. *(Jesus)

Mt 24:32 "Now learn this lesson from the fig tree: As soon as its twigs get tender and its leaves come out, you know that summer is near. [...]

Mt 24:33 [...] Even so, when you see all these things,* you know that it** is near, right at the door. *(#12 Mt 24:6 - Mt 24:26) **(the end)

Mk 13:28 "Now learn this lesson from the fig tree: As soon as its twigs get tender and its leaves come out, you know that summer is near. [...]

Mk 13:29 [...] Even so, when you see these things* happening, you know that it** is near, right at the door. *(#12 Mk 13:4 - Mk 13:21) **(the end)

Lk 21:31 Even so, when you see these things* happening, you know that the kingdom of God is near. *(#12 Lk 21:8, 21:9 & Lk 21:20) [...]

Lk 21:32 [...] "Truly I tell you, this generation will certainly not pass away until all these things have happened.

Jn 6:45   It is written in the Prophets: 'They will all be taught by God.' Everyone who has heard the Father and learned from him comes to me.

23. DO <u>LISTEN</u> / ACT ON GOD'S WORD

Mt 4:4	Jesus answered,* "It is written: 'Man shall not live on bread alone, but on every word that comes from the mouth of God.'" *(to the devil)
Mt 7:24	"Therefore everyone who hears these words of mine and puts them into practice is like a wise man who built his house on the rock.
Mt 7:26	But everyone who hears these words of mine and does not put them into practice is like a foolish man who built his house on sand.
Mt 10:14	If anyone will not welcome you or listen to your words, leave that home or town and shake the dust off your feet.
Mt 11:14	And if you are willing to accept it, he* is the Elijah who was to come. *(John the Baptist) [...]
Mt 11:15	[...] Whoever has ears, let them hear.
Mt 13:8	Still other seed fell on good soil, where it produced a crop—a hundred, sixty or thirty times what was sown. [...]
Mt 13:9	[...] Whoever has ears, let them hear." [...]
Mt 13:18	[...] "Listen then to what the parable of the sower means: [...]
Mt 13:23	[...] But the seed falling on good soil refers to someone who hears the word and understands it. This is the one who produces a crop, yielding a hundred, sixty or thirty times what was sown."

Mt 13:43	Then* the righteous will shine like the sun in the kingdom of their Father. Whoever has ears, let them hear. *(at the end of the age after the sinful are gone)
Mt 15:10	Jesus called the crowd to him and said, "Listen and understand. [...]
Mt 15:11	[...] What goes into someone's mouth does not defile them, but what comes out of their mouth, that is what defiles them."
Mt 17:5	While he was still speaking, a bright cloud covered them,* and a voice from the cloud said, "This is my Son, whom I love; with him I am well pleased. Listen to him!" *(Jesus and others)
Mk 4:3	"Listen! A farmer went out to sow his seed. [...]
Mk 4:8	[...] Still other seed fell on good soil. It came up, grew and produced a crop, some multiplying thirty, some sixty, some a hundred times." [...]
Mk 4:9	[...] Then Jesus said, "Whoever has ears to hear, let them hear." [...]
Mk 4:20	[...] Others, like seed sown on good soil, hear the word, accept it, and produce a crop—some thirty, some sixty, some a hundred times what was sown."
Mk 4:22	For whatever is hidden is meant to be disclosed, and whatever is concealed is meant to be brought out into the open. [...]
Mk 4:23	[...] If anyone has ears to hear, let them hear."
Mk 4:24	"Consider carefully what you hear," he continued. "With the measure you use, it will be measured to you—and even more.

Mk 7:14	Again Jesus called the crowd to him and said, "Listen to me, everyone, and understand this. [...]
Mk 7:15	[...] Nothing outside a person can defile them by going into them. Rather, it is what comes out of a person that defiles them."
Mk 9:7	Then a cloud appeared and covered them,* and a voice came from the cloud: "This is my Son, whom I love. Listen to him!" *(Jesus and others)
Mk 12:29	"The most important one,"* answered Jesus, "is this: 'Hear, O Israel: The Lord our God, the Lord is one. *(commandment) [...]
Mk 12:30	[...] Love the Lord your God with all your heart and with all your soul and with all your mind and with all your strength.' [...]
Mk 12:31	[...] The second is this: 'Love your neighbor as yourself.' There is no commandment greater than these." [...]
Mk 12:32	[...] "Well said, teacher," the man replied. "You are right in saying that God is one and there is no other but him.[...]
Mk 12:33	[...] To love him* with all your heart, with all your understanding and with all your strength, and to love your neighbor as yourself is more important than all burnt offerings and sacrifices." *(God) [...]
Mk 12:34	[...] When Jesus saw that he* had answered wisely, he said to him, "You are not far from the kingdom of God." And from then on no one dared ask him any more questions. *(a teacher of the law)

Lk 4:4	Jesus answered,* "It is written: 'Man shall not live on bread alone.' *(to the devil) [see Mt 4:4]
Lk 5:15	Yet the news about him spread all the more, so that crowds of people came to hear him and to be healed of their sicknesses.
Lk 6:27	"But to you who are listening I say: Love your enemies, do good to those who hate you, [...]
Lk 6:28	[...] bless those who curse you, pray for those who mistreat you.
Lk 6:47	As for everyone who comes to me and hears my words and puts them into practice, I will show you what they are like. [...]
Lk 6:48	[...] They* are like a man building a house, who dug down deep and laid the foundation on rock. When a flood came, the torrent struck that house but could not shake it, because it was well built. *(Lk 6:47)
Lk 6:49	But the one who hears my words and does not put them into practice is like a man who built a house on the ground without a foundation. The moment the torrent struck that house, it collapsed and its destruction was complete."
Lk 8:8	Still other seed fell on good soil. It came up and yielded a crop, a hundred times more than was sown." When he said this, he called out, "Whoever has ears to hear, let them hear." [...]
Lk 8:15	[...] But the seed on good soil stands for those with a noble and good heart, who hear the word, retain it, and by persevering produce a crop.

Lk 8:18	Therefore consider carefully how you listen. Whoever has will be given more; whoever does not have, even what they think they have will be taken from them."
Lk 8:21	He replied, "My mother and brothers are those who hear God's word and put it into practice."
Lk 9:35	A voice came from the cloud,* saying, "This is my Son, whom I have chosen; listen to him." *(over Jesus and others)
Lk 9:44	"Listen carefully to what I am about to tell you: The Son of Man is going to be delivered into the hands of men."
Lk 10:16	"Whoever listens to you listens to me; whoever rejects you rejects me; but whoever rejects me rejects him who sent me."
Lk 10:39	She* had a sister called Mary, who sat at the Lord's feet listening to what he said. *(Martha) [...]
Lk 10:40	[...] But Martha was distracted by all the preparations that had to be made. She came to him and asked, "Lord, don't you care that my sister has left me to do the work by myself? Tell her to help me!" [...]
Lk 10:41	[...] "Martha, Martha," the Lord answered, "you are worried and upset about many things, [...]
Lk 10:42	[...] but few things are needed—or indeed only one. Mary has chosen what is better, and it will not be taken away from her."
Lk 11:27	As Jesus was saying these things, a woman in the crowd called out, "Blessed is the mother who gave you birth and nursed you."[...]

Lk 11:28	[...] He replied, "Blessed rather are those who hear the word of God and obey it."
Lk 14:34	"Salt is good, but if it loses its saltiness, how can it be made salty again? [...]
Lk 14:35	[...] It* is fit neither for the soil nor for the manure pile; it is thrown out. "Whoever has ears to hear, let them hear." *(salt)
Lk 15:1	Now the tax collectors and sinners were all gathering around to hear Jesus.
Lk 18:5	yet because this widow keeps bothering me,* I will see that she gets justice, so that she won't eventually come and attack me!'" *(a judge) [...]
Lk 18:6	[...] And the Lord said, "Listen to what the unjust judge says.
Lk 21:38	and all the people came early in the morning to hear him at the temple.
Jn 5:24	"Very truly I tell you, whoever hears my word and believes him who sent me has eternal life and will not be judged but has crossed over from death to life.
Jn 6:45	It is written in the Prophets: 'They will all be taught by God.' Everyone who has heard the Father and learned from him comes to me.
Jn 8:31	To the Jews who had believed him, Jesus said, "If you hold to my teaching, you are really my disciples. [...]
Jn 8:32	[...] Then you will know the truth, and the truth will set you free."
Jn 8:51	Very truly I tell you, whoever obeys my word will never see death."

Jn 8:55   Though you do not know him,* I know him. If I said I did not, I would be a liar like you, but I do know him and obey his word. *(God)

Jn 10:27   My sheep listen to my voice; I know them, and they follow me.

Jn 11:42   I knew that you* always hear me, but I said this for the benefit of the people standing here,** that they may believe that you sent me." *(God) **(by Lazarus' tomb)

Jn 12:28   Father, glorify your name!" Then a voice came from heaven, "I have glorified it, and will glorify it again." [...]

Jn 12:30   [...] Jesus said, "This voice was for your* benefit, not mine. *(the crowd)

Jn 12:47   "If anyone hears my words but does not keep them, I do not judge that person. For I did not come to judge the world, but to save the world.

Jn 12:48   There is a judge for the one who rejects me and does not accept my words; the very words I have spoken will condemn them at the last day.

Jn 17:6   "I have revealed you* to those whom you gave me out of the world. They were yours; you gave them to me and they have obeyed your word. *(God)

Jn 17:8   For I gave them* the words you** gave me and they accepted them. They knew with certainty that I came from you, and they believed that you sent me. *(those in the world given by God to Jesus) **(God)

24. DO <u>LOVE GOD / LOVE JESUS</u>

Mt 3:17   And a voice from heaven said, "This* is my Son, whom I love; with him I am well pleased." *(at baptism of Jesus)

Mt 4:7   Jesus answered him,* "It is also written: 'Do not put the Lord your God to the test.' *(the devil who wanted him to throw himself down from the highest point of the temple to be aided by angels)

Mt 4:10   Jesus said to him, "Away from me, Satan! For it is written: 'Worship the Lord your God, and serve him only.'"

Mt 6:24   "No one can serve two masters. Either you will hate the one and love the other, or you will be devoted to the one and despise the other. You cannot serve both God and money.

Mt 6:33   But seek first his kingdom and his righteousness, and all these things will be given to you as well.

Mt 9:8   When the crowd saw this,* they were filled with awe; and they praised God, who had given such authority to man. *(that Jesus had cured a man and forgiven his sins)

Mt 10:37   "Anyone who loves their father or mother more than me is not worthy of me; anyone who loves their son or daughter more than me is not worthy of me.

Mt 11:6	Blessed is anyone who does not stumble on account of me."
Mt 11:25	At that time Jesus said, "I praise you, Father, Lord of heaven and earth, because you have hidden these things from the wise and learned, and revealed them to little children.
Mt 14:33	Then those who were in the boat worshiped* him, saying, "Truly you are the Son of God." *(for saving drowning Peter and calming the wind)
Mt 15:31	The people were amazed when they saw the mute speaking, the crippled made well, the lame walking and the blind seeing. And they praised the God of Israel.
Mt 22:21	"Caesar's,"* they** replied. Then he said to them, "So give back to Caesar what is Caesar's, and to God what is God's." *(concerning whose image was on a coin) **(disciples of the Pharisees with the Herodians)
Mt 22:37	Jesus replied:* "'Love the Lord your God with all your heart and with all your soul and with all your mind.' *(to an expert in the law) [...]
Mt 22:38	[...] This is the first and greatest commandment. [...]
Mt 22:39	[...] And the second is like it: 'Love your neighbor as yourself.' [...]
Mt 22:40	[...] All the Law and the Prophets hang on these two commandments."
Mt 23:8	"But you are not to be called 'Rabbi,' for you have one Teacher, and you are all brothers.
Mt 23:9	And do not call anyone on earth 'father,' for you have one Father, and he is in heaven.

Mt 23:10 Nor are you to be called instructors, for you have one Instructor, the Messiah.

Mt 26:13 Truly I tell you, wherever this gospel is preached throughout the world, what she* has done will also be told, in memory of her." *(a woman who poured perfume on Jesus' body)

Mk 1:11 And a voice came from heaven: "You are my Son, whom I love; with you I am well pleased."

Mk 2:12 He* got up, took his mat and walked out in full view of them all. This amazed everyone and they praised God, saying, "We have never seen anything like this!" *(paralyzed man)

Mk 9:7 Then a cloud appeared and covered them,* and a voice came from the cloud: "This is my Son, whom I love. Listen to him!" *(Jesus and others)

Mk 12:17 Then Jesus said to them,* "Give back to Caesar what is Caesar's and to God what is God's." And they were amazed at him. *(Pharisees and Herodians asking if they should pay taxes)

Mk 12:29 "The most important one,"* answered Jesus,** "is this: 'Hear, O Israel: The Lord our God, the Lord is one. *(commandment) **(to a teacher of the law) [...]

Mk 12:30 [...] Love the Lord your God with all your heart and with all your soul and with all your mind and with all your strength.' [...]

Mk 12:31 [...] The second is this: 'Love your neighbor as yourself.' There is no commandment greater than these." [...]

Mk 12:32	[...] "Well said, teacher," the man replied. "You are right in saying that God is one and there is no other but him.[...]
Mk 12:33	[...] To love him* with all your heart, with all your understanding and with all your strength, and to love your neighbor as yourself is more important than all burnt offerings and sacrifices." *(God) [...]
Mk 12:34	[...] When Jesus saw that he* had answered wisely, he said to him, "You are not far from the kingdom of God." And from then on no one dared ask him any more questions. *(a teacher of the law)
Mk 12:44	They* all gave out of their wealth; but she,** out of her poverty, put in*** everything— all she had to live on." *(many rich people) **(a poor widow) ***(donating to the temple treasury)
Mk 14:9	Truly I tell you, wherever the gospel is preached throughout the world, what she* has done will also be told, in memory of her." (a woman who poured perfume on Jesus' body)
Lk 1:46	And Mary said: "My soul glorifies the Lord [...}
Lk 1:47	[...]and my spirit rejoices in God my Savior, [...]
Lk 1:49	[...] for the Mighty One has done great things for me— holy is his name.
Lk 1:64	Immediately his* mouth was opened and his tongue set free, and he began to speak, praising God. *(Zechariah at the birth of his son, John the Baptist)

Lk 1:68	"Praise* be to the Lord, the God of Israel, because he has come to his people and redeemed them. *(Song of Zechariah, father of John the Baptist)
Lk 2:14	"Glory* to God in the highest heaven, and on earth peace to those on whom his favor rests." *(said by angels at time of birth of Jesus)
Lk 2:20	The shepherds returned, glorifying and praising God for all the things* they had heard and seen, which were just as they had been told. *(at the time of Jesus birth)
Lk 2:37	and then was a widow* until she was eighty-four. She never left the temple but worshiped night and day, fasting and praying. *(Anna, a prophet)
Lk 3:21	When all the people were being baptized, Jesus was baptized too. And as he was praying, heaven was opened [...]
Lk 3:22	[...]and the Holy Spirit descended on him in bodily form like a dove. And a voice came from heaven: "You are my Son, whom I love; with you I am well pleased."
Lk 4:8	Jesus answered,* "It is written: 'Worship the Lord your God and serve him only.'" *(to the devil)
Lk 4:12	Jesus answered,* "It is said: 'Do not put the Lord your God to the test.'" *(to the devil who wanted him to throw himself down from the highest point of the temple to be aided by angels)

Lk 5:25	Immediately he* stood up in front of them, took what he had been lying on and went home praising God. *(a paralyzed man who was cured) [...]
Lk 5:26	[...] Everyone was amazed and gave praise to God. They were filled with awe and said, "We have seen remarkable things today."
Lk 7:16	They* were all filled with awe and praised God. "A great prophet has appeared among us," they said. "God has come to help his people." *(the people of Nain, a crowd and his disciples)
Lk 7:23	Blessed is anyone who does not stumble on account of me."
Lk 7:44	Then he turned toward the woman* and said to Simon, "Do you see this woman? I came into your house. You did not give me any water for my feet, but she wet my feet with her tears and wiped them with her hair. *(a sinful woman) [...]
Lk 7:45	[...]You did not give me a kiss, but this woman, from the time I entered, has not stopped kissing my feet. [...]
Lk 7:46	[...] You did not put oil on my head, but she has poured perfume on my feet. [...]
Lk 7:47	[...] Therefore, I tell you, her* many sins have been forgiven—as her great love has shown. But whoever has been forgiven little loves little." *(a woman who kissed and wiped Jesus' feet) [...]

Lk 8:38	The man from whom the demons had gone out begged to go with him, but Jesus sent him away, saying, [...}
Lk 8:39	[...] "Return home and tell how much God has done for you." So the man went away and told all over town how much Jesus had done for him.
Lk 10:21	At that time Jesus, full of joy through the Holy Spirit, said, "I praise you, Father, Lord of heaven and earth, because you have hidden these things from the wise and learned, and revealed them to little children. Yes, Father, for this is what you were pleased to do.
Lk 10:27	He* answered, "'Love the Lord your God with all your heart and with all your soul and with all your strength and with all your mind'; and, 'Love your neighbor as yourself.'" *(an expert in the law who asked how to gain eternal life) [...]
Lk 10:28	[...] "You have answered correctly," Jesus replied. "Do this and you will live."
Lk 11:42	"Woe to you Pharisees, because you give God a tenth of your mint, rue and all other kinds of garden herbs, but you neglect justice and the love of God. You should have practiced the latter without leaving the former undone.
Lk 12:21	"This* is how it will be with whoever stores up things for themselves but is not rich toward God." *(like a dying man who cannot take his possessions with him)

Lk 12:31	But seek his kingdom, and these things will be given to you as well.
Lk 13:13	Then he put his hands on her,* and immediately she straightened up and praised God. *(a crippled woman)
Lk 16:13	"No one can serve two masters. Either you will hate the one and love the other, or you will be devoted to the one and despise the other. You cannot serve both God and money."
Lk 17:15	One of them,* when he saw he was healed, came back, praising God in a loud voice. *(of ten men with leprosy) [...]
Lk 17:18	[...] Has* no one** returned to give praise to God except this foreigner?"*** *(Jesus said) **(of the other nine cured) ***(a Samaritan)
Lk 18:43	Immediately he* received his sight and followed Jesus, praising God. When all the people saw it, they also praised God. *(a blind man)
Lk 19:37	When he came near the place where the road goes down the Mount of Olives, the whole crowd of disciples began joyfully to praise God in loud voices for all the miracles they had seen:
Lk 20:25	He said to them,* "Then give back to Caesar what is Caesar's, and to God what is God's." *(spies of the teachers of the law and the chief priests who asked if they should pay taxes)
Lk 21:4	All these people gave their gifts out of their wealth; but she* out of her poverty put in** all she had to live on." *(a poor widow) **(to the temple collection)

Lk 23:46	Jesus called out with a loud voice, "Father, into your hands I commit my spirit." When he had said this, he breathed his last.
Lk 24:52	Then they* worshiped him** and returned to Jerusalem with great joy. *(the disciples) **(Jesus)
Lk 24:53	And they* stayed continually at the temple, praising God. *(the disciples)
Jn 4:23	Yet a time is coming and has now come when the true worshipers will worship the Father in the Spirit and in truth, for they are the kind of worshipers the Father seeks. [...]
Jn 4:24	[...] God is spirit, and his worshipers must worship in the Spirit and in truth."
Jn 5:22	Moreover, the Father judges no one, but has entrusted all judgment to the Son, [...]
Jn 5:23	[...] that all may honor the Son just as they honor the Father. Whoever does not honor the Son does not honor the Father, who sent him.
Jn 9:38	Then the man* said, "Lord, I believe," and he worshiped him. *(born blind and cured)
Jn 14:15	"If you love me, keep my commands.
Jn 14:21	Whoever has my commands and keeps them is the one who loves me. The one who loves me will be loved by my Father, and I too will love them and show myself to them."
Jn 14:23	Jesus replied,* "Anyone who loves me will obey my teaching. My Father will love them, and we will come to them and make our home with them. *(to Judas, not Judas Iscariot)

Jn 14:28	"You heard me say, 'I am going away and I am coming back to you.' If you loved me, you would be glad that I am going to the Father, for the Father is greater than I.
Jn 14:31	but he* comes so that the world may learn that I love the Father and do exactly what my Father has commanded me. "Come now; let us leave. *(the prince of this world)
Jn 15:8	This is to my Father's glory, that you bear much fruit, showing yourselves to be my disciples.
Jn 15:9	"As the Father has loved me, so have I loved you. Now remain in my love.
Jn 15:10	If you keep my commands, you will remain in my love, just as I have kept my Father's commands and remain in his love.
Jn 15:16	You did not choose me, but I chose you and appointed you so that you might go and bear fruit—fruit that will last*—and so that whatever you ask in my name the Father will give you. *(our gift to God)
Jn 16:27	No, the Father himself loves you because you have loved me and have believed that I came from God.
Jn 17:1	After Jesus said this,* he looked toward heaven and prayed: "Father, the hour has come. Glorify your Son, that your Son may glorify you. *("I have overcome the world.")

Jn 21:15	When they had finished eating, Jesus said to Simon Peter, "Simon son of John, do you love me more than these?" "Yes, Lord," he said, "you know that I love you." Jesus said, "Feed my lambs." [...]
Jn 21:16	[...] Again Jesus said, "Simon son of John, do you love me?" He answered, "Yes, Lord, you know that I love you." Jesus said, "Take care of my sheep." [...]
Jn 21:17	[...] The third time he said to him, "Simon son of John, do you love me?" Peter was hurt because Jesus asked him the third time, "Do you love me?" He said, "Lord, you know all things; you know that I love you." Jesus said, "Feed my sheep.

25. DO <u>LOVE YOUR NEIGHBOR</u>

Mt 5:22   But I tell you that anyone who is angry with a brother or sister, will be subject to judgment. Again, anyone who says to a brother or sister, 'Raca,' is answerable to the court. And anyone who says, 'You fool!' will be in danger of the fire of hell.

Mt 5:39   But I tell you, do not resist an evil person. If anyone slaps you on the right cheek, turn to them the other cheek also.

Mt 5:40   And if anyone wants to sue you and take your shirt, hand over your coat as well.

Mt 5:41   If anyone forces you to go one mile, go with them two miles.

Mt 5:42   Give to the one who asks you, and do not turn away from the one who wants to borrow from you.

Mt 5:44   But I tell you, love your enemies and pray for those who persecute you,

Mt 6:2   "So when you give to the needy, do not announce it with trumpets, as the hypocrites do in the synagogues and on the streets, to be honored by others. Truly I tell you, they have received their reward in full.

Mt 6:3   But when you give to the needy, do not let your left hand know what your right hand is doing, [...]

Mt 6:4	[...] so that your giving may be in secret. Then your Father, who sees what is done in secret, will reward you.
Mt 7:12	So in everything, do to others what you would have them do to you, for this sums up the Law and the Prophets.
Mt 10:14	If anyone will not welcome you or listen to your words, leave that home or town and shake the dust off your feet.
Mt 10:40	"Anyone who welcomes you welcomes me, and anyone who welcomes me welcomes the one who sent me.
Mt 10:41	Whoever welcomes a prophet as a prophet will receive a prophet's reward, and whoever welcomes a righteous person as a righteous person will receive a righteous person's reward.
Mt 10:42	And if anyone gives even a cup of cold water to one of these little ones who is my disciple, truly I tell you, that person will certainly not lose their reward."
Mt 18:5	And whoever welcomes one such child in my name welcomes me.
Mt 18:10	"See that you do not despise one of these little ones. For I tell you that their angels in heaven always see the face of my Father in heaven.
Mt 19:14	Jesus said, "Let the little children come to me, and do not hinder them, for the kingdom of heaven belongs to such as these."
Mt 19:16	Just then a man* came up to Jesus and asked, "Teacher, what good thing must I do to get eternal life?" *(wealthy) [...]

Mt 19:19	[…] honor your father and mother,' and 'love your neighbor as yourself.'" […]
Mt 19:21	[…] Jesus answered, "If you* want to be perfect, go, sell your possessions and give to the poor, and you will have treasure in heaven. Then come, follow me." *(a wealthy man with many possessions who had kept all God's commandments)
Mt 20:28	just as the Son of Man did not come to be served, but to serve, and to give his life as a ransom for many."
Mt 22:21	"Caesar's,"* they** replied. Then he said to them, "So give back to Caesar what is Caesar's, and to God what is God's." *(concerning whose image was on a coin) **(disciples of the Pharisees with the Herodians)
Mt 22:37	Jesus replied:* "'Love the Lord your God with all your heart and with all your soul and with all your mind.' *(to an expert in the law) […]
Mt 22:38	[…] This is the first and greatest commandment. […]
Mt 22:39	[…] And the second is like it: 'Love your neighbor as yourself.' […]
Mt 22:40	[…] All the Law and the Prophets hang on these two commandments."
Mt 25:40	"The King* will reply, 'Truly I tell you,** whatever you did for one of the least of these brothers and sisters of mine, you did for me.' *(the Son of Man) **(the righteous on his right) […]

Mt 25:45	[...] "He* will reply, 'Truly I tell you,** whatever you did not do for one of the least of these, you did not do for me.' *(the King-the Son of Man) **(to the accursed on his left) [...]
Mt 25:46	[...] "Then they* will go away to eternal punishment, but the righteous** to eternal life." *(Mt 25:45) **(Mt 25:40)
Mk 4:24	"Consider carefully what you hear," he continued. "With the measure you use, it will be measured to you—and even more.
Mk 6:11	And if any place will not welcome* you or listen to you, leave that place and shake the dust off your feet as a testimony against them." *(receive)
Mk 7:21	For it is from within, out of a person's heart, that evil thoughts come—sexual immorality, theft, murder, [...]
Mk 7:22	[...] adultery, greed, malice, deceit, lewdness, envy, slander, arrogance and folly. [...]
Mk 7:23	[...] All these* evils come from inside and defile a person." *(Mk 7:21 and Mk 7:22)
Mk 9:37	"Whoever welcomes* one of these little children in my name welcomes me; and whoever welcomes me does not welcome me but the one who sent me." *(receives)
Mk 9:41	Truly I tell you, anyone who gives you a cup of water in my name because you belong to the Messiah will certainly not lose their reward.
Mk 10:13	People were bringing little children to Jesus for him to place his hands on them, but the disciples rebuked them. [...]

Mk 10:14   [...] When Jesus saw this,* he was indignant. He said to them, "Let the little children come to me, and do not hinder them, for the kingdom of God belongs to such as these. *(Mk 10:13)

Mk 10:15   Truly I tell you, anyone who will not receive the kingdom of God like a little child will never enter it."

Mk 10:21   Jesus looked at him* and loved him. "One thing you lack," he said. "Go, sell everything you have and give to the poor, and you will have treasure in heaven. Then come, follow me." *(a wealthy man who had kept all of God's commandments who wanted to know how to inherit eternal life)

Mk 12:17   Then Jesus said to them,* "Give back to Caesar what is Caesar's and to God what is God's." And they were amazed at him. *(Pharisees and Herodians asking if they should pay taxes)

Mk 12:29   "The most important one,"* answered Jesus,** "is this: 'Hear, O Israel: The Lord our God, the Lord is one.*(commandment) **(to a teacher of the law) [...]

Mk 12:30   [...] Love the Lord your God with all your heart and with all your soul and with all your mind and with all your strength.' [...]

Mk 12:31   [...] The second is this: 'Love your neighbor as yourself.' There is no commandment greater than these." [...]

Mk 12:32   [...] "Well said, teacher," the man replied. "You are right in saying that God is one and there is no other but him. [...]

Mk 12:33	[...] To love him* with all your heart, with all your understanding and with all your strength, and to love your neighbor as yourself is more important than all burnt offerings and sacrifices." *(God) [...]
Mk 12:34	[...] When Jesus saw that he* had answered wisely, he said to him, "You are not far from the kingdom of God." And from then on no one dared ask him any more questions. *(a teacher of the law)
Lk 6:27	"But to you who are listening I say: Love your enemies, do good to those who hate you, [...]
Lk 6:28	[...] bless those who curse you, pray for those who mistreat you.
Lk 6:29	If someone slaps you on one cheek, turn to them the other also. If someone takes your coat, do not withhold your shirt from them.
Lk 6:30	Give to everyone who asks you, and if anyone takes what belongs to you, do not demand it back.
Lk 6:31	Do to others as you would have them do to you.
Lk 6:35	But love your enemies, do good to them, and lend to them without expecting to get anything back. Then your reward will be great, and you will be children of the Most High, because he is kind to the ungrateful and wicked.
Lk 6:38	Give, and it will be given to you. A good measure, pressed down, shaken together and running over, will be poured into your lap. For with the measure you use, it will be measured to you."

Lk 9:11   but the crowds learned about it* and followed him. He welcomed them and spoke to them about the kingdom of God, and healed those who needed healing. *(that Jesus and the apostles had withdrawn to Bethsaida)

Lk 10:27   He* answered, "'Love the Lord your God with all your heart and with all your soul and with all your strength and with all your mind'; and, 'Love your neighbor as yourself.'" *(an expert in the law who asked how to inherit eternal life) [...]

Lk 10:28   [...] "You have answered correctly," Jesus replied. "Do this and you will live."

Lk 10:36   "Which of these three* do you think was a neighbor to the man who fell into the hands of robbers?" *(two not helpful walkers and one helpful walker) [...]

Lk 10:37   [...] The expert in the law replied, "The one who had mercy on him." Jesus told him, "Go and do likewise."

Lk 11:13   If you then, though you are evil, know how to give good gifts to your children, how much more will your Father in heaven give the Holy Spirit to those who ask him!"

Lk 11:41   But now as for what is inside you—be generous to the poor, and everything will be clean for you.

Lk 12:33   Sell your possessions and give to the poor. Provide purses for yourselves that will not wear out, a treasure in heaven that will never fail, where no thief comes near and no moth destroys.

Lk 14:13	But when you give a banquet, invite the poor, the crippled, the lame, the blind, [...]
Lk 14:14	[...] and you will be blessed. Although they cannot repay you, you will be repaid at the resurrection of the righteous."
Lk 18:16	But Jesus called the children to him and said, "Let the little children come to me, and do not hinder them, for the kingdom of God belongs to such as these.
Lk 18:22	When Jesus heard this,* he said to him,** "You still lack one thing. Sell everything you have and give to the poor, and you will have treasure in heaven. Then come, follow me." *(the question of how one should inherit eternal life if he has obeyed all the commandments since his youth) **(a wealthy ruler)
Lk 20:25	He said to them,* "Then give back to Caesar what is Caesar's, and to God what is God's." *(spies of the teachers of the law and the chief priests who asked if they should pay taxes)
Lk 23:28	Jesus turned and said to them,* "Daughters of Jerusalem, do not weep for me; weep for yourselves and for your children. *(those following him on the way to his crucifixion)
Jn 13:15	I have set you an example that you should do as I have done for you.
Jn 13:20	Very truly I tell you, whoever accepts anyone I send accepts me; and whoever accepts me accepts the one who sent me."

Jn 13:34	"A new command I give you: Love one another. As I have loved you, so you must love one another.
Jn 14:27	Peace I leave with you; my peace I give you. I do not give to you as the world gives. Do not let your hearts be troubled and do not be afraid.
Jn 15:12	My command is this: Love each other as I have loved you.
Jn 15:13	Greater love has no one than this: to lay down one's life for one's friends.
Jn 15:17	This is my command: Love each other.

26. DO <u>LOVE YOURSELF</u>

Mt 19:19	honor your father and mother,' and 'love your neighbor as yourself.'"
Mt 22:37	Jesus replied: "'Love the Lord your God with all your heart and with all your soul and with all your mind.' *(to an expert in the law) [...]
Mt 22:38	[...] This is the first and greatest commandment. [...]
Mt 22:39	[...] And the second is like it: 'Love your neighbor as yourself.' [...]
Mt 22:40	[...] All the Law and the Prophets hang on these two commandments."
Mk 12:29	"The most important one,"* answered Jesus,** "is this: 'Hear, O Israel: The Lord our God, the Lord is one. *(commandment) **(to a teacher of the law) [...]
Mk 12:30	[...] Love the Lord your God with all your heart and with all your soul and with all your mind and with all your strength.' [...]
Mk 12:31	[...] The second is this: 'Love your neighbor as yourself.' There is no commandment greater than these." [...]
Mk 12:32	[...] "Well said, teacher," the man replied. "You are right in saying that God is one and there is no other but him. [...]

Mk 12:33   […] To love him* with all your heart, with all your understanding and with all your strength, and to love your neighbor as yourself is more important than all burnt offerings and sacrifices." *(God) […]

Mk 12:34   […] When Jesus saw that he* had answered wisely, he said to him, "You are not far from the kingdom of God." And from then on no one dared ask him any more questions. *(a teacher of the law)

Lk 10:27   He* answered, "'Love the Lord your God with all your heart and with all your soul and with all your strength and with all your mind'; and, 'Love your neighbor as yourself.'" *(an expert in the law who asked how to inherit eternal life) […]

Lk 10:28   […] "You have answered correctly," Jesus replied. "Do this and you will live."

Lk 11:35   See to it, then, that the light within you is not darkness.

27. DO ACCEPT PERSECUTION

Mt 5:10	Blessed are those who are persecuted because of righteousness, for theirs is the kingdom of heaven.
Mt 5:11	"Blessed are you when people insult you, persecute you and falsely say all kinds of evil against you because of me. [...]
Mt 5:12	[...] Rejoice and be glad, because great is your reward in heaven, for in the same way they persecuted the prophets who were before you.
Mt 5:44	But I tell you, love your enemies and pray for those who persecute you,
Mt 10:23	When you are persecuted in one place, flee to another. Truly I tell you, you will not finish going through the towns of Israel before the Son of Man comes.
Mt 10:39	Whoever finds their life will lose it, and whoever loses their life for my sake will find it.
Mt 13:21	But since they* have no root, they last only a short time. When trouble or persecution comes because of the word, they quickly fall away. *(people like seed on rocky ground)
Mt 16:25	For whoever wants to save their life will lose it, but whoever loses their life for me will find it.
Mt 24:9	"Then you will be handed over to be persecuted and put to death, and you will be hated by all nations because of me.

Mk 4:17   But since they* have no root, they last only a short time. When trouble or persecution comes because of the word, they quickly fall away. *(people like seed on rocky ground)

Mk 8:35   For whoever wants to save their life will lose it, but whoever loses their life for me and for the gospel will save it.

Mk 10:29   "Truly I tell you," Jesus replied, "no one who has left home or brothers or sisters or mother or father or children or fields for me and the gospel [...]

Mk 10:30   [...] will fail to receive a hundred times as much in this present age: homes, brothers, sisters, mothers, children and fields—along with persecutions—and in the age to come eternal life.

Lk 9:24   For whoever wants to save their life will lose it, but whoever loses their life for me will save it.

Lk 17:33   Whoever tries to keep their life will lose it, and whoever loses their life will preserve it.

Jn 10:11   "I am the good shepherd. The good shepherd lays down his life for the sheep.

Jn 10:15   just as the Father knows me and I know the Father—and I lay down my life for the sheep.

Jn 10:17   The reason my Father loves me is that I lay down my life—only to take it up again. [...]

Jn 10:18   [...] No one takes it from me, but I lay it down of my own accord. I have authority to lay it down and authority to take it up again. This command I received from my Father."

Jn 12:25	Anyone who loves their life will lose it, while anyone who hates their life in this world will keep it for eternal life.
Jn 15:13	Greater love has no one than this: to lay down one's life for one's friends.
Jn 15:20	Remember what I told you: 'A servant is not greater than his master.' If they persecuted me, they will persecute you also. If they obeyed my teaching, they will obey yours also.

28. DO <u>PERSEVERE</u>

Mt 10:22   You will be hated by everyone because of me, but the one who stands firm to the end will be saved.

Mt 13:21   But since they* have no root, they last only a short time. When trouble or persecution comes because of the word, they quickly fall away. *(people like seed on rocky ground) [same wording as Mk 4:17]

Mt 24:13   but the one who stands firm to the end will be saved.

Mk 4:17   But since they* have no root, they last only a short time. When trouble or persecution comes because of the word, they quickly fall away. *(people like seed on rocky ground) [Same wording as Mt 13:21]

Mk 9:50   "Salt is good, but if it loses its saltiness, how can you make it salty again? Have salt among yourselves, and be at peace with each other."

Mk 13:13   Everyone will hate you because of me, but the one who stands firm to the end will be saved.

Lk 8:15   But the seed on good soil stands for those with a noble and good heart, who hear the word, retain it, and by persevering produce a crop.

Lk 11:8	I tell you,* even though he** will not get up and give you the bread because of friendship, yet because of your shameless audacity he will surely get up and give you as much as you need. *(if you persevere in asking) **(the neighbor)
Lk 14:34	"Salt is good, but if it loses its saltiness, how can it be made salty again? [...]
Lk 14:35	[...] It* is fit neither for the soil nor for the manure pile; it is thrown out. "Whoever has ears to hear, let them hear." *(salt)
Lk 18:1	Then Jesus told his disciples a parable* to show them that they should always pray and not give up. *(about a widow who requests repeatedly) [...]
Lk 18:5	[...] yet because this widow keeps bothering me,* I will see that she gets justice, so that she won't eventually come and attack me!'" *(a judge) [...]
Lk 18:6	[...] And the Lord said, "Listen to what the unjust judge says. [...]
Lk 18:7	[...] And will not God bring about justice for his chosen ones, who cry out to him day and night? Will he keep putting them off? [...]
Lk 18:8	[...] I tell you, he will see that they get justice, and quickly. However, when the Son of Man comes, will he find faith on the earth?"
Lk 21:19	Stand firm, and you will win life.

Jn 15:4   Remain in me, as I also remain in you. No branch can bear fruit by itself; it must remain in the vine. Neither can you bear fruit unless you remain in me.

Jn 15:5   "I am the vine; you are the branches. If you remain in me and I in you, you will bear much fruit; apart from me you can do nothing.

Jn 15:7   If you remain in me and my words remain in you, ask whatever you wish, and it will be done for you.

Jn 15:9   "As the Father has loved me, so have I loved you. Now remain in my love.

Jn 15:10   If you keep my commands, you will remain in my love, just as I have kept my Father's commands and remain in his love.

29. DO PRAY / ASK

Mt 5:44	But I tell you, love your enemies and pray for those who persecute you,
Mt 6:5	"And when you pray, do not be like the hypocrites, for they love to pray standing in the synagogues and on the street corners to be seen by others. Truly I tell you, they have received their reward in full.
Mt 6:6	But when you pray, go into your room, close the door and pray to your Father, who is unseen. Then your Father, who sees what is done in secret, will reward you.
Mt 6:7	And when you pray, do not keep on babbling like pagans, for they think they will be heard because of their many words.[...]
Mt 6:8	[...] Do not be like them,* for your Father knows what you need before you ask him. *(the pagans)
Mt 6:9	"This, then, is how you should pray: "'Our Father in heaven, hallowed by your name, [see Appendix B for complete prayer]
Mt 7:7	"Ask and it will be given to you; seek and you will find; knock and the door will be opened to you.
Mt 7:11	If you, then, though you are evil, know how to give good gifts to your children, how much more will your Father in heaven give good gifts to those who ask him!

Mt 9:38	Ask the Lord of the harvest, therefore, to send out workers into his harvest field."
Mt 14:23	After he had dismissed them, he went up on a mountainside by himself to pray. Later that night, he was there alone,
Mt 18:19	"Again, truly I tell you that if two of you on earth agree about anything they ask for, it will be done for them by my Father in heaven.
Mt 19:13	Then people brought little children to Jesus for him to place his hands on them and pray for them. But the disciples rebuked them.* *(Jesus stopped the disciples)
Mt 21:22	If you believe, you will receive whatever you ask for in prayer."
Mt 24:20	Pray that your flight* will not take place in winter or on the Sabbath. *(in end times)
Mt 26:36	Then Jesus went with his disciples to a place called Gethsemane, and he said to them, "Sit here while I go over there and pray."
Mt 26:39	Going a little farther, he fell with his face to the ground and prayed, "My Father, if it is possible, may this cup be taken from me. Yet not as I will, but as you will."
Mt 26:41	"Watch and pray so that you will not fall into temptation. The spirit is willing, but the flesh is weak."
Mt 26:42	He went away a second time and prayed, "My Father, if it is not possible for this cup to be taken away unless I drink it, may your will be done."

Mt 26:44	So he left them* and went away once more and prayed the third time, saying the same thing** *(his disciples) **(Mt 26:42)
Mk 1:35	Very early in the morning, while it was still dark, Jesus got up, left the house and went off to a solitary place, where he prayed.
Mk 6:46	After leaving them, he went up on a mountainside to pray.
Mk 9:29	He replied, "This kind* can come out only by prayer." *(an impure spirit)
Mk 11:24	Therefore I tell you, whatever you ask for in prayer, believe that you have received it, and it will be yours.
Mk 11:25	And when you stand praying, if you hold anything against anyone, forgive them, so that your Father in heaven may forgive you your sins."
Mk 12:40	They* devour widows' houses and for a show make lengthy prayers. These men will be punished most severely." *(teachers of the law)
Mk 13:18	Pray that this* will not take place in winter, *(the end)
Mk 14:32	They went to a place called Gethsemane, and Jesus said to his disciples, "Sit here while I pray."
Mk 14:35	Going a little farther, he fell to the ground and prayed that if possible the hour might pass from him.
Mk 14:38	Watch and pray so that you will not fall into temptation. The spirit is willing, but the flesh is weak."

Mk 14:39	Once more he went away and prayed the same thing.* *(Mk 14:35)
Lk 2:37	and then was a widow* until she was eighty-four. She never left the temple but worshiped night and day, fasting and praying. *(Anna, a prophet)
Lk 3:21	When all the people were being baptized, Jesus was baptized too. And as he was praying, heaven was opened [...]
Lk 3:22	[...] and the Holy Spirit descended on him in bodily form like a dove. And a voice came from heaven: "You are my Son, whom I love; with you I am well pleased."
Lk 5:16	But Jesus often withdrew to lonely places and prayed.
Lk 6:12	One of those days Jesus went out to a mountainside to pray, and spent the night praying to God.
Lk 6:27	"But to you who are listening I say: Love your enemies, do good to those who hate you, [...]
Lk 6:28	[...] bless those who curse you, pray for those who mistreat you.
Lk 9:18	Once when Jesus was praying in private and his disciples were with him, he asked them, "Who do the crowds say I am?"
Lk 9:28	About eight days after Jesus said this,* he took Peter, John and James with him and went up onto a mountain to pray. *(Some will not taste death until they see the kingdom of God) [...]

Lk 9:29	[...] As he was praying, the appearance of his face changed, and his clothes became as bright as a flash of lightning.
Lk 10:2	He told them,* "The harvest is plentiful, but the workers are few. Ask the Lord of the harvest, therefore, to send out workers into his harvest field. *(the seventy-two appointed to proceed him)
Lk 11:1	One day Jesus was praying in a certain place. When he finished, one of his disciples said to him, "Lord, teach us to pray, just as John taught his disciples." [...]
Lk 11:2	[...] He said to them,* "When you pray, say: "'Father, hallowed be your name, your kingdom come. *(the disciples) [See Appendix B for complete prayer.]
Lk 11:9	"So I say to you: Ask and it will be given to you; seek and you will find; knock and the door will be opened to you. [...]
Lk 11:10	[...] For everyone who asks receives; the one who seeks finds; and to the one who knocks, the door will be opened.
Lk 11:13	If you then, though you are evil, know how to give good gifts to your children, how much more will your Father in heaven give the Holy Spirit to those who ask him!"
Lk 18:1	Then Jesus told his disciples a parable* to show them that they should always pray and not give up. *(about a widow who requests repeatedly) [...]

Lk 18:5   [...] yet because this widow keeps bothering me,* I will see that she gets justice, so that she won't eventually come and attack me!'" *(a judge) [...]

Lk 18:6   [...] And the Lord said, "Listen to what the unjust judge says. [...]

Lk 18:7   [...] And will not God bring about justice for his chosen ones, who cry out to him day and night? Will he keep putting them off? [...]

Lk 18:8   [...] I tell you, he will see that they get justice, and quickly. However, when the Son of Man comes, will he find faith on the earth?"

Lk 18:10   "Two men went up to the temple to pray, one a Pharisee and the other a tax collector. [...]

Lk 18:14   [...] "I tell you that this man,* rather than the other,** went home justified before God. For all those who exalt themselves will be humbled, and those who humble themselves will be exalted." *(a humble tax collector who asked for mercy) **(a proud Pharisee who praised himself)

Lk 21:36   Be always on the watch, and pray that you may be able to escape all that is about to happen, and that you may be able to stand before the Son of Man."

Lk 22:32   But I have prayed for you, Simon, that your faith may not fail. And when you have turned back, strengthen your brothers."

Lk 22:40   On reaching the place,* he said to them,** "Pray that you will not fall into temptation." *(Mount of Olives) **(the disciples)

Lk 22:41	He withdrew about a stone's throw beyond them,* knelt down and prayed, *(the disciples) [...]
Lk 22:42	[...] "Father, if you are willing, take this cup from me; yet not my will, but yours be done."
Lk 22:44	And being in anguish, he prayed more earnestly, and his sweat was like drops of blood falling to the ground.
Lk 22:46	"Why are you sleeping?" he asked them.* "Get up and pray so that you will not fall into temptation." *(the disciples)
Lk 23:46	Jesus called out with a loud voice, "Father, into your hands I commit my spirit." When he had said this, he breathed his last.
Jn 14:13	And I will do whatever you ask in my name, so that the Father may be glorified in the Son.
Jn 14:14	You may ask me for anything in my name, and I will do it.
Jn 15:7	If you remain in me and my words remain in you, ask whatever you wish, and it will be done for you.
Jn 15:16	You did not choose me, but I chose you and appointed you so that you might go and bear fruit––fruit that will last––and so that whatever you ask in my name the Father will give you.
Jn 16:23	In that day* you will no longer ask me anything. Very truly I tell you, my Father will give you whatever you ask in my name. *(when I see you again)

Jn 16:24	Until now you have not asked for anything in my name. Ask and you will receive, and your joy will be complete.
Jn 17:1	After Jesus said this,* he looked toward heaven and prayed: "Father, the hour has come. Glorify your Son, that your Son may glorify you. *("I have overcome the world.")
Jn 17:9	I pray for them. I am not praying for the world, but for those you have given me, for they are yours.
Jn 17:15	My prayer is not that you* take them** out of the world but that you protect them from the evil one. *(God) **(those God gave Jesus)
Jn 17:20	"My prayer is not for them* alone. I pray also for those who will believe in me through their message, *(those in the world given by God to Jesus)

30. DO **PREPARE** / KEEP WATCH

Mt 24:42	"Therefore keep watch, because you do not know on what day your Lord will come.
Mt 24:43	But understand this: If the owner of the house had known at what time of night the thief was coming, he would have kept watch and would not have let his house be broken into. [...]
Mt 24:44	[...] So you also must be ready, because the Son of Man will come at an hour when you do not expect him.
Mt 24:46	It will be good for that servant whose master finds him doing so* when he returns. *(being faithful)
Mt 24:50	The master of that servant* will come on a day when he does not expect him and at an hour he is not aware of. *(who beats fellow servants and eats with drunkards)
Mt 25:13	"Therefore keep watch, because you do not know the day or the hour.* (of the coming of the Son of Man)
Mt 26:38	Then he said to them,* "My soul is overwhelmed with sorrow to the point of death. Stay here and keep watch with me." *(the disciples)
Mt 26:41	"Watch and pray so that you will not fall into temptation. The spirit is willing, but the flesh is weak."

Mk 13:33	Be on guard! Be alert! You do not know when that time will come.
Mk 13:35	"Therefore keep watch because you do not know when the owner* of the house will come back—whether in the evening, or at midnight, or when the rooster crows, or at dawn. *(the Son of Man)
Mk 13:36	If he* comes suddenly, do not let him find you sleeping. *(the owner of the house - the Son of Man)
Mk 13:37	[...] What I say to you, I say to everyone: 'Watch!'"
Mk 14:34	"My soul is overwhelmed with sorrow to the point of death," he said to them.* "Stay here and keep watch." *(Peter, James and John)
Mk 14:38	Watch and pray so that you will not fall into temptation. The spirit is willing, but the flesh is weak."
Lk 12:36	like servants* waiting for their master to return from a wedding banquet, so that when he comes and knocks they can immediately open the door for him. *(who are dressed with lamps burning) [...]
Lk 12:37	[...] It will be good for those servants whose master finds them watching when he comes. Truly I tell you, he will dress himself to serve, will have them recline at the table and will come and wait on them. [...]
Lk 12:38	[...] It will be good for those servants whose master finds them ready, even if he comes in the middle of the night or toward daybreak.

151

Lk 12:40	You also* must be ready, because the Son of Man will come at an hour when you do not expect him." *(like vigilant servants)
Lk 12:43	It will be good for that servant whom the master finds doing so* when he returns. *(being faithful)
Lk 12:46	The master of that servant* will come on a day when he does not expect him and at an hour he is not aware of. He will cut him to pieces and assign him a place with the unbelievers. *(who beats others and is drunk)
Lk 12:47	"The servant who knows the master's will and does not get ready or does not do what the master wants will be beaten with many blows. [...]
Lk 12:48	[...] But the one who does not know and does things deserving punishment will be beaten with few blows. From everyone who has been given much, much will be demanded; and from the one who has been entrusted with much, much more will be asked.
Lk 17:3	So watch yourselves. "If your brother or sister sins against you, rebuke them; and if they repent, forgive them.
Lk 21:36	Be always on the watch, and pray that you may be able to escape all that is about to happen, and that you may be able to stand before the Son of Man."

31. DO **REBUKE** WRONGDOERS

Mt 7:5   You hypocrite, first take the plank out of your own eye, and then you will see clearly to remove the speck from your brother's eye.

Mt 18:15   "If your brother or sister sins, go and point out their fault, just between the two of you. If they listen to you, you have won them over. [...]

Mt 18:16   [...] But if they* will not listen, take one or two others along, so that 'every matter may be established by the testimony of two or three witnesses.' *(your brother or sister) [...]

Mt 18:17   [...] If they* still refuse to listen, tell it to the church; and if they refuse to listen even to the church, treat them as you would a pagan or a tax collector. *(your brother or sister)

Mt 21:12   Jesus entered the temple courts and drove out all who were buying and selling there. He overturned the tables of the money changers and the benches of those selling doves.

Mk 16:14   Later Jesus appeared to the Eleven as they were eating; he rebuked them for their lack of faith and their stubborn refusal to believe those who had seen him after he had risen.

Lk 6:42	How can you say to your brother, 'Brother, let me take the speck out of your eye,' when you yourself fail to see the plank in your own eye? You hypocrite, first take the plank out of your eye, and then you will see clearly to remove the speck from your brother's eye.
Lk 9:55	But Jesus turned and rebuked them.* (James and John who reacted to Samaritans who would not welcome them since they were on their way to Jerusalem)
Lk 17:3	So watch yourselves. "If your brother or sister sins against you, rebuke them; and if they repent, forgive them.
Jn 2:15	So he made a whip out of cords, and drove all from the temple courts, both sheep and cattle; he scattered the coins of the money changers and overturned their tables. [...]
Jn 2:16	[...] To those who sold doves he said, "Get these out of here! Stop turning my Father's house into a market!"

32. DO <u>REPENT</u> / BE RECONCILED

Mt 4:17   From that time on Jesus began to preach, "Repent, for the kingdom of heaven has come near."

Mt 5:23   "Therefore, if you are offering your gift at the altar and there remember that your brother or sister has something against you, [...]

Mt 5:24   [...] leave your gift there in front of the altar. First go and be reconciled to them;* then come and offer your gift. *(your brother of sister)

Mt 5:25   "Settle matters quickly with your adversary who is taking you to court. Do it while you are still together on the way, or your adversary may hand you over to the judge, and the judge may hand you over to the officer, and you may be thrown into prison.

Mt 7:5   You hypocrite, first take the plank out of your own eye, and then you will see clearly to remove the speck from your brother's eye.

Mt 11:20   Then Jesus began to denounce the towns in which most of his miracles had been performed, because they did not repent.

Mt 11:21   "Woe to you, Chorazin! Woe to you, Bethsaida! For if the miracles that were performed in you had been performed in Tyre and Sidon, they would have repented long ago in sackcloth and ashes.

Mt 21:32	For John came to you* to show you the way of righteousness, and you did not believe him, but the tax collectors and the prostitutes did. And even after you saw this, you did not repent and believe him. *(chief priests and elders of the people)
Mk 1:15	"The time has come," he said. "The kingdom of God has come near. Repent and believe the good news!"
Lk 5:32	I have not come to call the righteous, but sinners to repentance."
Lk 6:42	How can you say to your brother, 'Brother, let me take the speck out of your eye,' when you yourself fail to see the plank in your own eye? You hypocrite, first take the plank out of your eye, and then you will see clearly to remove the speck from your brother's eye.
Lk 12:58	As you are going with your adversary to the magistrate, try hard to be reconciled on the way, or your adversary may drag you off to the judge, and the judge turn you over to the officer, and the officer throw you into prison.
Lk 13:3	I tell you, no! But unless you repent, you too will all perish. [same wording as Lk 13:5]
Lk 13:5	I tell you, no! But unless you repent, you too will all perish." [same wording as Lk 13:3]
Lk 15:7	I tell you that in the same way* there will be more rejoicing in heaven over one sinner who repents than over ninety-nine righteous persons who do not need to repent. *(as a man who found a lost lamb)

Lk 15:10   In the same way,* I tell you, there is rejoicing
              in the presence of the angels of God over one
              sinner who repents." *(as a woman who found
              a lost coin)

Lk 17:3   So watch yourselves. "If your brother or sister
              sins against you, rebuke them; and if they
              repent, forgive them.

Lk 17:4   Even if they* sin against you seven times in a
              day and seven times come back to you saying
              'I repent,' you must forgive them." *(your
              brother or sister)

Lk 24:47   and* repentance for the forgiveness of sins
              will be preached in his name to all nations,
              beginning at Jerusalem. *(he said that it is
              written that)

33. DO REGARDING <u>SACRAMENTS</u>

Mt 3:15	Jesus replied, "Let it* be so now; it is proper for us to do this to fulfill all righteousness." Then John consented. *(to baptize Jesus)
Mt 16:19	I will give you* the keys of the kingdom of heaven; whatever you bind on earth will be bound in heaven, and whatever you loose on earth will be loosed in heaven." *(Peter)
Mt 18:18	"Truly I tell you, whatever you bind on earth will be bound in heaven, and whatever you loose on earth will be loosed in heaven.
Mt 26:26	While they were eating, Jesus took bread, and when he had given thanks, he broke it and gave it to his disciples, saying, "Take and eat; this is my body." [...]
Mt 26:27	[...] Then he took a cup, and when he had given thanks, he gave it to them, saying, "Drink from it, all of you. [...]
Mt 26:28	[...] This is my blood of the covenant, which is poured out for many for the forgiveness of sins.
Mt 28:19	Therefore go and make disciples of all nations, baptizing them in the name of the Father and of the Son and of the Holy Spirit,
Mk 1:9	At that time Jesus came from Nazareth in Galilee and was baptized by John in the Jordan.

Mk 14:22	While they* were eating, Jesus took bread, and when he had given thanks, he broke it and gave it to his disciples, saying, "Take it; this is my body." *(Jesus and the twelve) [...]
Mk 14:23	[...] Then he took a cup, and when he had given thanks, he gave it to them,* and they all drank from it. *(the disciples)
Mk 16:16	Whoever believes and is baptized will be saved, but whoever does not believe will be condemned.
Lk 3:21	When all the people were being baptized, Jesus was baptized too. And as he was praying, heaven was opened [...]
Lk 3:22	[...] and the Holy Spirit descended on him in bodily form like a dove. And a voice came from heaven: "You are my Son, whom I love; with you I am well pleased."
Lk 22:17	After taking the cup, he gave thanks and said, "Take this and divide it among you.* *(the apostles) [...]
Lk 22:19	[...] And he took bread, gave thanks and broke it, and gave it to them,* saying, "This is my body given for you; do this in remembrance of me." *(the apostles) [...]
Lk 22:20	[...] In the same way, after the supper he took the cup, saying, "This cup is the new covenant in my blood, which is poured out for you.
Jn 3:5	Jesus answered, "Very truly I tell you, no one can enter the kingdom of God unless they are born of water and the Spirit.

Jn 3:22	After this, Jesus and his disciples went out into the Judean countryside, where he spent some time with them, and baptized.
Jn 3:26	They came to John and said to him, "Rabbi, that man who was with you on the other side of the Jordan—the one you testified about—look, he is baptizing, and everyone is going to him."
Jn 4:1	Now Jesus learned that the Pharisees had heard that he was gaining and baptizing more disciples than John- [...]
Jn 4:2	[...] although in fact it was not Jesus who baptized, but his disciples. [...]
Jn 6:27	Do not work for food that spoils, but for food that endures to eternal life, which the Son of Man will give you. For on him God the Father has placed his seal of approval."
Jn 6:51	I am the living bread that came down from heaven. Whoever eats this bread will live forever. This bread is my flesh, which I will give for the life of the world."
Jn 6:53	Jesus said to them, "Very truly I tell you, unless you eat the flesh of the Son of Man and drink his blood, you have no life in you.
Jn 6:54	Whoever eats my flesh and drinks my blood has eternal life, and I will raise them up at the last day.
Jn 6:56	Whoever eats my flesh and drinks my blood remains in me, and I in them.

Jn 6:57	Just as the living Father sent me and I live because of the Father, so the one who feeds on me will live because of me.
Jn 6:58	This is the bread that came down from heaven. Your ancestors ate manna and died, but whoever feeds on this bread will live forever."
Jn 14:16	And I will ask the Father, and he will give you another advocate to help you and be with you forever— [...]
Jn 14:17	[...] the Spirit of truth. The world cannot accept him, because it neither sees him nor knows him. But you know him, for he lives with you and will be in you.
Jn 20:21	Again Jesus said, "Peace be with you! As the Father has sent me, I am sending you."* *(the disciples) [...]
Jn 20:22	[...] And with that he breathed on them and said, "Receive the Holy Spirit.
Jn 20:23	If you* forgive anyone's sins, their sins are forgiven; if you do not forgive them, they are not forgiven." *(the disciples)

34. DO BE A GOOD <u>SERVANT</u> / SLAVE

Mt 20:26   Not so* with you.** Instead, whoever wants to become great among you must be your servant, *(like the Gentiles and their high officials who exercise authority over them) **(the twelve)

Mt 20:27   and whoever wants to be first must be your slave––

Mt 20:28   just as the Son of Man did not come to be served, but to serve, and to give his life as a ransom for many."

Mt 23:11   The greatest among you will be your servant.

Mt 24:46   It will be good for that servant whose master finds him doing so* when he returns. *(being faithful)

Mk 9:35   Sitting down, Jesus called the Twelve and said, "Anyone who wants to be first must be the very last, and the servant of all."

Mk 10:43   Not so* with you.** Instead, whoever wants to become great among you must be your servant. *(like the Gentiles and their high officials who exercise authority over them) **(the twelve)

Mk 10:44   and whoever wants to be first must be slave of all.

Mk 10:45   For even the Son of Man did not come to be served, but to serve, and to give his life as a ransom for many."

Lk 19:17   "'Well done, my good servant!' his master replied. 'Because you have been trustworthy in a very small matter, take charge of ten cities.' [...]

Lk 19:19   [...] "His master answered,* 'You take charge of five cities.' *(to another faithful servant)

Lk 22:26   But you are not to be like that. Instead, the greatest among you should be like the youngest, and the one who rules like the one who serves. [...]

Lk 22:27   [...] For who is greater, the one who is at the table or the one who serves? Is it not the one who is at the table? But I am among you as one who serves.

Jn 12:26   Whoever serves me must follow me; and where I am, my servant also will be. My Father will honor the one who serves me.

Jn 13:16   Very truly I tell you, no servant is greater than his master, nor is a messenger greater than the one who sent him. [...]

Jn 13:17   [...] Now that you know these things,* you will be blessed if you do them. *(Jesus examples)

35. DO PROPER SPEECH / THOUGHTS

Mt 5:8	Blessed are the pure in heart, for they will see God
Mt 5:22	But I tell you that anyone who is angry with a brother or sister will be subject to judgment. Again, anyone who says to a brother or sister, 'Raca,' is answerable to the court. And anyone who says, 'You fool!' will be in danger of the fire of hell.
Mt 5:34	But I tell you, do not swear an oath at all: either by heaven, for it is God's throne; [...]
Mt 5:35	[...] or by the earth, for it is his footstool; or by Jerusalem, for it is the city of the Great King.
Mt 5:36	And do not swear by your head, for you cannot make even one hair white or black.
Mt 5:37	All you need to say is simply 'Yes' or 'No'; anything beyond this comes from the evil one.
Mt 10:19	But when they arrest you, do not worry about what to say or how to say it. At that time you will be given what to say,
Mt 10:27	What I tell you in the dark, speak in the daylight; what is whispered in your ear, proclaim from the roofs.
Mt 11:25	At that time Jesus said, "I praise you, Father, Lord of heaven and earth, because you have hidden these things from the wise and learned, and revealed them to little children.

Mt 12:36	But I tell you that everyone will have to give account on the day of judgment for every empty word they have spoken.
Mt 12:37	For by your words you will be acquitted, and by your words you will be condemned."
Mt 15:10	Jesus called the crowd to him and said, "Listen and understand. [...]
Mt 15:11	[...] What goes into someone's mouth does not defile them, but what comes out of their mouth, that is what defiles them."
Mt 15:18	But the things that come out of a person's mouth come from the heart, and these defile them.
Mt 15:19	For out of the heart come evil thoughts— murder, adultery, sexual immorality, theft, false testimony, slander. [...]
Mt 15:20	[...] These* are what defile a person; but eating with unwashed hands does not defile them." *(Mt 15:19)
Mt 23:20	Therefore, anyone who swears by the altar swears by it and by everything on it.
Mt 23:21	And anyone who swears by the temple swears by it and by the one who dwells in it.
Mt 23:22	And anyone who swears by heaven swears by God's throne and by the one who sits on it.
Mk 7:14	Again Jesus called the crowd to him and said, "Listen to me, everyone, and understand this. [...]
Mk 7:15	[...] Nothing outside a person can defile them by going into them. Rather, it is what comes out of a person that defiles them."

Mk 7:21	For it is from within, out of a person's heart, that evil thoughts come—sexual immorality, theft, murder, [...]
Mk 7:22	[...] adultery, greed, malice, deceit, lewdness, envy, slander, arrogance and folly. [...]
Mk 7:23	[...] All these* evils come from inside and defile a person." *(Mk 7:21 and Mk 7:22)
Mk 13:11	Whenever you are arrested and brought to trial, do not worry beforehand about what to say. Just say whatever is given you at the time, for it is not you speaking, but the Holy Spirit.
Lk 1:51	He* has performed mighty deeds with his arm; he has scattered those who are proud in their inmost thoughts. *(God)
Lk 6:45	A good man brings good things out of the good stored up in his heart, and an evil man brings evil things out of the evil stored up in his heart. For the mouth speaks what the heart is full of.
Lk 12:11	"When you are brought before synagogues, rulers and authorities, do not worry about how you will defend yourselves or what you will say, [...]
Lk 12:12	[...] for the Holy Spirit will teach you at that time what you should say."
Lk 21:14	But* make up your mind not to worry beforehand how you will defend yourselves. *(when you are seized during end times) [...]
Lk 21:15	[...] For I will give you words and wisdom that none of your adversaries will be able to resist or contradict.

Jn 6:43   "Stop grumbling among yourselves,"* Jesus answered. *(some Jews)

Also see #5 Don't Blasheme

36. DO <u>TEACH</u> / PREACH

Mt 4:17	From that time on Jesus began to preach, "Repent, for the kingdom of heaven has come near."
Mt 4:23	Jesus went throughout Galilee, teaching in their synagogues, proclaiming the good news of the kingdom, and healing every disease and sickness among the people.
Mt 5:19	Therefore anyone who sets aside one of the least of these commands and teaches others accordingly will be called least in the kingdom of heaven, but whoever practices and teaches these commands will be called great in the kingdom of heaven.
Mt 7:28	When Jesus had finished saying these things,* the crowds were amazed at his teaching, *(#23 Mt 7:24 and Mt 7:26) […]
Mt 7:29	[…] because he taught as one who had authority, and not as their teachers of the law.
Mt 9:35	Jesus went through all the towns and villages, teaching in their synagogues, proclaiming the good news of the kingdom and healing every disease and sickness.
Mt 11:1	After Jesus had finished instructing his twelve disciples, he went on from there to teach and preach in the towns of Galilee.

Mt 13:54	Coming to his hometown, he began teaching the people in their synagogue, and they were amazed. "Where did this man get this wisdom and these miraculous powers?" they asked.
Mt 21:23	Jesus entered the temple courts, and, while he was teaching, the chief priests and the elders of the people came to him. "By what authority are you doing these things?" they asked. "And who gave you this authority?"* *(He did not respond)
Mt 22:16	They* sent their disciples to him along with the Herodians. "Teacher," they said, "we know that you are a man of integrity and that you teach the way of God in accordance with the truth. You aren't swayed by others, because you pay no attention to who they are. *(the Pharisees)
Mt 22:33	When the crowds heard this,* they were astonished at his teaching. *(story of a woman with seven husbands)
Mt 26:55	In that hour Jesus said to the crowd, "Am I leading a rebellion, that you have come out with swords and clubs to capture me? Every day I sat in the temple courts teaching, and you did not arrest me.
Mt 28:19	Therefore go and make disciples of all nations, baptizing them in the name of the Father and of the Son and of the Holy Spirit, [...]
Mt 28:20	[...] and teaching them* to obey everything I have commanded you. And surely I am with you always, to the very end of the age." *(disciples of all nations)

Mk 1:14	After John was put in prison, Jesus went into Galilee, proclaiming the good news of God.
Mk 1:21	They* went to Capernaum, and when the Sabbath came, Jesus went into the synagogue and began to teach. *(Jesus and his followers)
Mk 1:38	Jesus replied,* "Let us go somewhere else—to the nearby villages—so I can preach there also. That is why I have come." *(to Simon and his companions)
Mk 1:39	So he traveled throughout Galilee, preaching in their synagogues and driving out demons.
Mk 2:2	They* gathered in such large numbers that there was no room left, not even outside the door, and he preached the word to them. *(the people of Capernaum)
Mk 2:13	Once again Jesus went out beside the lake. A large crowd came to him, and he began to teach them.
Mk 3:14	He appointed twelve that they might be with him and that he might send them out to preach
Mk 4:1	Again Jesus began to teach by the lake. The crowd that gathered around him was so large that he got into a boat and sat in it out on the lake, while all the people were along the shore at the water's edge.
Mk 4:33	With many similar parables Jesus spoke the word to them,* as much as they could understand. *(the crowd)

Mk 6:2   When the Sabbath came, he began to teach in the synagogue, and many who heard him were amazed. "Where did this man get these things?" they asked. "What's this wisdom that has been given him? What are these remarkable miracles he is performing?

Mk 6:6   He was amazed at their* lack of faith. Then Jesus went around teaching from village to village. *(people in his own town)

Mk 6:34   When Jesus landed and saw a large crowd, he had compassion on them, because they were like sheep without a shepherd. So he began teaching them many things.

Mk 8:31   He then began to teach them* that the Son of Man must suffer many things and be rejected by the elders, the chief priests and the teachers of the law, and that he must be killed and after three days rise again. *(his disciples)

Mk 9:31   because he was teaching his disciples. He said to them, "The Son of Man is going to be delivered into the hands of men. They will kill him, and after three days he will rise."

Mk 10:1   Jesus then left that place and went into the region of Judea and across the Jordan. Again crowds of people came to him, and as was his custom, he taught them.

Mk 11:17 And as he taught them,* he said, "Is it not written: 'My house will be called a house of prayer for all nations'? But you have made it 'a den of robbers.'" *(those buying and selling in the temple) [...]

Mk 11:18   [...] The chief priests and the teachers of the law heard this* and began looking for a way to kill him, for they feared him, because the whole crowd was amazed at his teaching. *(that he had driven out those selling in the temple)

Mk 12:14   They* came to him and said, "Teacher, we know that you are a man of integrity. You aren't swayed by others, because you pay no attention to who they are; but you teach the way of God in accordance with the truth. Is it right to pay the imperial tax to Caesar or not? *(the Pharisees and Herodians)

Mk 12:35   While Jesus was teaching in the temple courts, he asked, "Why do the teachers of the law say that the Messiah is the son of David?

Mk 12:38   As he taught, Jesus said, "Watch out for the teachers of the law. They like to walk around in flowing robes and be greeted with respect in the marketplaces, [...]

Mk 12:39   [...] and have the most important seats in the synagogues and the places of honor at banquets. [...]

Mk 12:40   [...] They* devour widows' houses and for a show make lengthy prayers. These men will be punished most severely." *(teachers of the law)

Mk 14:49   Every day I was with you,* teaching in the temple courts, and you did not arrest me. But the Scriptures must be fulfilled." *(a crowd sent from the chief priests, the teachers of the law and the elders)

Mk 16:15	He said to them, "Go into all the world and preach the gospel to all creation.
Lk 3:3	He* went into all the country around the Jordan, preaching a baptism of repentance for the forgiveness of sins. *(John the Baptist)
Lk 4:15	He was teaching in their* synagogues, and everyone praised him. *(those in Galilee)
Lk 4:16	He went to Nazareth, where he had been brought up, and on the Sabbath day he went into the synagogue, as was his custom. He stood up to read, [...]
Lk 4:17	[...] and the scroll of the prophet Isaiah was handed to him. Unrolling it, he found the place where it is written: [...]
Lk 4:18	[...] "The Spirit of the Lord is on me, because he has anointed me to proclaim good news to the poor. He has sent me to proclaim freedom for the prisoners and recovery of sight for the blind, to set the oppressed free, [...]
Lk 4:19	[...] to proclaim the year of the Lord's favor." [...]
Lk 4:20	[...] Then he rolled up the scroll, gave it back to the attendant and sat down. The eyes of everyone in the synagogue were fastened on him. [...]
Lk 4:21	[...] He began by saying to them, "Today this scripture is fulfilled in your hearing."
Lk 4:31	Then he went down to Capernaum, a town in Galilee, and on the Sabbath he taught the people.
Lk 4:32	They* were amazed at his teaching, because his words had authority. *(people of Capernaum)

Lk 4:43	But he said, "I must proclaim the good news of the kingdom of God to the other towns also, because that is why I was sent."
Lk 4:44	And he kept on preaching in the synagogues of Judea.
Lk 5:3	He got into one of the boats, the one belonging to Simon, and asked him to put out a little from shore. Then he sat down and taught the people from the boat.
Lk 5:15	Yet the news about him spread all the more, so that crowds of people came to hear him and to be healed of their sicknesses.
Lk 5:17	One day Jesus was teaching, and Pharisees and teachers of the law were sitting there. They had come from every village of Galilee and from Judea and Jerusalem. And the power of the Lord was with Jesus to heal the sick.
Lk 6:6	On another Sabbath he went into the synagogue and was teaching, and a man was there whose right hand was shriveled.* *(he cured him)
Lk 7:1	When Jesus had finished saying all this* to the people who were listening, he entered Capernaum. *(see App F Lk 5:36 – Lk 6:47-49)
Lk 7:24	After John's messengers left, Jesus began to speak to the crowd about John: "What did you go out into the wilderness to see? A reed swayed by the wind?
Lk 8:1	After this, Jesus traveled about from one town and village to another, proclaiming the good news of the kingdom of God. The Twelve were with him,

Lk 9:2	and he sent them* out to proclaim the kingdom of God and to heal the sick. *(the twelve)
Lk 9:6	So they* set out and went from village to village, proclaiming the good news and healing people everywhere. *(the twelve)
Lk 9:11	but the crowds learned about it* and followed him. He welcomed them and spoke to them about the kingdom of God, and healed those who needed healing. *(that Jesus and the twelve had withdrawn to Bethsaida)
Lk 9:59	He said to another man, "Follow me." But he replied, "Lord, first let me go and bury my father." [...]
Lk 9:60	[...] Jesus said to him, "Let the dead bury their own dead, but you go and proclaim the kingdom of God."
Lk 10:3	Go! I am sending you out like lambs among wolves.
Lk 10:8	"When you enter a town and are welcomed, eat what is offered to you. [...]
Lk 10:9	[...] Heal the sick who are there and tell them, 'The kingdom of God has come near to you.' [...]
Lk 10:10	[...] But when you enter a town and are not welcomed, go into its streets and say, [...]
Lk 10:11	[...] 'Even the dust of your town we wipe from our feet as a warning to you. Yet be sure of this: The kingdom of God has come near.'
Lk 13:10	On a Sabbath Jesus was teaching in one of the synagogues,

Lk 13:22   Then Jesus went through the towns and villages, teaching as he made his way to Jerusalem

Lk 19:47   Every day he was teaching at the temple. But the chief priests, the teachers of the law and the leaders among the people were trying to kill him.

Lk 20:1   One day as Jesus was teaching the people in the temple courts and proclaiming the good news, the chief priests and the teachers of the law, together with the elders, came up to him.

Lk 20:21   So the spies questioned him: "Teacher, we know that you speak and teach what is right, and that you do not show partiality but teach the way of God in accordance with the truth.

Lk 21:37   Each day Jesus was teaching at the temple, and each evening he went out to spend the night on the hill called the Mount of Olives,

Lk 22:32   But I have prayed for you, Simon, that your faith may not fail. And when you have turned back, strengthen your brothers."

Lk 23:5   But they* insisted, "He stirs up the people all over Judea by his teaching. He started in Galilee and has come all the way here."** *(the chief priests and the crowd) **(Jerusalem)

Lk 24:47   and* repentance for the forgiveness of sins will be preached in his name to all nations, beginning at Jerusalem. *(he said that it is written that)

Jn 3:2	He* came to Jesus at night and said, "Rabbi, we know that you are a teacher who has come from God. For no one could perform the signs you are doing if God were not with him." *(Nicodemus, a Pharisee)
Jn 6:45	It is written in the Prophets: 'They will all be taught by God.' Everyone who has heard the Father and learned from him comes to me.
Jn 6:59	He said this* while teaching in the synagogue in Capernaum. *(eat and drink of the Son of Man)
Jn 7:14	Not until halfway through the festival did Jesus go up to the temple courts and begin to teach.
Jn 7:16	Jesus answered, "My teaching is not my own. It comes from the one who sent me.
Jn 7:28	Then Jesus, still teaching in the temple courts, cried out, "Yes, you know me, and you know where I am from. I am not here on my own authority, but he* who sent me is true. You do not know him, *(God) [...]
Jn 7:29	[...]but I know him* because I am from him and he sent me." *(God)
Jn 8:2	At dawn he appeared again in the temple courts, where all the people gathered around him, and he sat down to teach them.
Jn 8:12	When Jesus spoke again to the people, he said, "I am the light of the world. Whoever follows me will never walk in darkness, but will have the light of life."

Jn 8:20	He spoke these words* while teaching in the temple courts near the place where the offerings were put. Yet no one seized him, because his hour had not yet come. *(You do not know me or the Father)
Jn 13:13	"You call me 'Teacher' and 'Lord,' and rightly so, for that is what I am.
Jn 15:27	And you also must testify, for you have been with me from the beginning.
Jn 18:20	"I have spoken openly to the world," Jesus replied. "I always taught in synagogues or at the temple, where all the Jews come together. I said nothing in secret.
Jn 20:21	Again Jesus said, "Peace be with you! As the Father has sent me, I am sending you."* *(the disciples)

37. DO GIVE <u>THANKS</u> / ASK BLESSING

Mt 14:19   And he directed the people to sit down on the grass. Taking the five loaves and the two fish and looking up to heaven, he gave thanks and broke the loaves. Then he gave them to the disciples, and the disciples gave them to the people.* *(there was food remaining after feeding 5000 men besides women and children)

Mt 15:36   Then he took the seven loaves and the fish, and when he had given thanks, he broke them and gave them to the disciples, and they in turn to the people.* *(there was food remaining after feeding 4000 men besides women and children)

Mt 26:26   While they were eating, Jesus took bread, and when he had given thanks, he broke it and gave it to his disciples, saying, "Take and eat; this is my body."

Mt 26:27   Then he took a cup, and when he had given thanks, he gave it to them, saying, "Drink from it, all of you. [...]

Mt 26:28   [...] This is my blood of the covenant, which is poured out for many for the forgiveness of sins.

Mk 6:41   Taking the five loaves and the two fish and looking up to heaven, he gave thanks and broke the loaves. Then he gave them to his disciples to distribute to the people. He also divided the two fish among them all.* *(there was food remaining after feeding 5000 men)

Mk 8:6	He told the crowd to sit down on the ground. When he had taken the seven loaves and given thanks, he broke them and gave them to his disciples to distribute to the people, and they did so. [...]
Mk 8:7	[...] They* had a few small fish as well; he gave thanks for them also and told the disciples to distribute them.** *(the disciples) **(there was food remaining after feeding 4000)
Mk 14:22	While they* were eating, Jesus took bread, and when he had given thanks, he broke it and gave it to his disciples, saying, "Take it; this is my body." *(Jesus and the twelve) [...]
Mk 14:23	[...] Then he took a cup, and when he had given thanks, he gave it to them,* and they all drank from it. *(the twelve)
Lk 2:38	Coming up to them* at that very moment, she** gave thanks to God and spoke about the child*** to all who were looking forward to the redemption of Jerusalem. *(Jesus, Mary and Joseph) **(Anna, a prophet) ***(Jesus)
Lk 5:25	Immediately he* stood up in front of them, took what he had been lying on and went home praising God. *(a paralyzed man who was cured)
Lk 9:16	Taking the five loaves and the two fish and looking up to heaven, he gave thanks and broke them. Then he gave them to the disciples to distribute to the people.* *(there was food remaining after feeding 5000 men)

Lk 10:20	However, do not rejoice that the spirits submit to you, but rejoice that your names are written in heaven."
Lk 13:13	Then he put his hands on her,* and immediately she straightened up and praised God. *(a crippled woman)
Lk 17:16	He threw himself at Jesus' feet and thanked him*––and he was a Samaritan. *(for being cured) [...]
Lk 17:18	[...] Has* no one** returned to give praise to God except this foreigner?"*** *(Jesus said) **(of the other nine cured) ***(a Samaritan)
Lk 18:43	Immediately he* received his sight and followed Jesus, praising God. When all the people saw it, they also praised God. *(a blind man)
Lk 19:37	When he came near the place where the road goes down the Mount of Olives, the whole crowd of disciples began joyfully to praise God in loud voices for all the miracles they had seen:
Lk 22:17	After taking the cup, he gave thanks and said, "Take this and divide it among you.* *(the apostles) [...]
Lk 22:19	[...] And he took bread, gave thanks and broke it, and gave it to them,* saying, "This is my body given for you; do this in remembrance of me." *(the apostles)
Lk 24:30	When he was at the table with them,* he took bread, gave thanks, broke it and began to give it to them. *(the two who had been on the road to Emmaus with him)

Lk 24:50	When he had led them out to the vicinity of Bethany, he lifted up his hands and blessed them.
Jn 6:11	Jesus then took the loaves, gave thanks, and distributed to those who were seated as much as they wanted. He did the same with the fish.* *(there was food remaining after feeding 5000 men)
Jn 6:23	Then some boats from Tiberias landed near the place where the people had eaten the bread after the Lord had given thanks.
Jn 11:41	So they took away the stone.* Then Jesus looked up and said, "Father, I thank you that you have heard me. *(at the tomb of Lazarus)

38. DO **TREAT THINGS** RESPECTFULLY

Mt 7:6   "Do not give dogs what is sacred; do not throw your pearls to pigs. If you do, they may trample them under their feet, and turn and tear you to pieces.

Mt 15:26   He replied, "It is not right to take the children's bread and toss it to the dogs."

Mt 21:12   Jesus entered the temple courts and drove out all who were buying and selling there. He overturned the tables of the money changers and the benches of those selling doves.

Mk 7:27   "First let the children eat all they want," he told her,* "for it is not right to take the children's bread and toss it to the dogs." *(a Greek woman with a daughter having an impure spirit)

Mk 11:15   On reaching Jerusalem, Jesus entered the temple courts and began driving out those who were buying and selling there. He overturned the tables of the money changers and the benches of those selling doves, [...]

Mk 11:16   [...] and would not allow anyone to carry merchandise through the temple courts.

Lk 16:9   I tell you, use worldly wealth to gain friends for yourselves, so that when it is gone, you will be welcomed into eternal dwellings.

Lk 16:10	"Whoever can be trusted with very little can also be trusted with much, and whoever is dishonest with very little will also be dishonest with much.
Lk 16:11	So if you have not been trustworthy in handling worldly wealth, who will trust you with true riches?
Lk 16:12	And if you have not been trustworthy with someone else's property, who will give you property of your own?
Lk 19:17	"'Well done, my good servant!' his master replied. 'Because you have been trustworthy in a very small matter, take charge of ten cities.' [...]
Lk 19:19	[...] "His master answered,* 'You take charge of five cities.' *(to another faithful servant)
Lk 19:45	When Jesus entered the temple courts, he began to drive out those who were selling.
Jn 2:15	So he made a whip out of cords, and drove all from the temple courts, both sheep and cattle; he scattered the coins of the money changers and overturned their tables.
Jn 2:16	To those who sold doves he said, "Get these out of here! Stop turning my Father's house into a market!"

39. DO GOD'S <u>WILL</u>

Mt 7:21   "Not everyone who says to me, 'Lord, Lord,' will enter the kingdom of heaven, but only the one who does the will of my Father who is in heaven.

Mt 11:25   At that time Jesus said, "I praise you, Father, Lord of heaven and earth, because you have hidden these things from the wise and learned, and revealed them to little children. [...]

Mt 11:26   [...] Yes, Father, for this* is what you were pleased to do. *(your will)

Mt 12:50   For whoever does the will of my Father in heaven is my brother and sister and mother."

Mt 26:39   Going a little farther, he fell with his face to the ground and prayed, "My Father, if it is possible, may this cup be taken from me. Yet not as I will, but as you will."

Mt 26:42   He went away a second time and prayed, "My Father, if it is not possible for this cup to be taken away unless I drink it, may your will be done."

Mt 26:44   So he left them* and went away once more and prayed the third time, saying the same thing** *(his disciples) **(Mt 26:42)

Mk 3:35   Whoever does God's will is my brother and sister and mother."

Mk 14:36   "Abba, Father," he said, "everything is possible for you. Take this cup from me. Yet not what I will, but what you will."

Lk 12:47	"The servant who knows the master's will and does not get ready or does not do what the master wants will be beaten with many blows. [...]
Lk 12:48	[...] But the one who does not know and does things deserving punishment will be beaten with few blows. From everyone who has been given much, much will be demanded; and from the one who has been entrusted with much, much more will be asked.
Lk 22:42	"Father, if you are willing, take this cup from me; yet not my will, but yours be done."
Jn 4:34	"My food," said Jesus, "is to do the will of him who sent me and to finish his work.
Jn 5:30	By myself I can do nothing; I judge only as I hear, and my judgment is just, for I seek not to please myself but him who sent me.
Jn 6:38	For I have come down from heaven not to do my will but to do the will of him who sent me.
Jn 6:39	And this is the will of him who sent me, that I shall lose none of all those he has given me, but raise them up at the last day.
Jn 6:40	For my Father's will is that everyone who looks to the Son and believes in him shall have eternal life, and I will raise them up at the last day."
Jn 7:17	Anyone who chooses to do the will of God will find out whether my teaching comes from God or whether I speak on my own.
Jn 8:28	So Jesus said, "When you have lifted up the Son of Man, then you will know that I am he and that I do nothing on my own but speak just what the Father has taught me. [...]

Jn 8:29   [...] The one who sent me is with me; he has not left me alone, for I always do what pleases him."

Jn 9:31   We* know that God does not listen to sinners. He listens to the godly person who does his will. *(a man cured of blindness and the people)

Jn 14:31   but he* comes so that the world may learn that I love the Father and do exactly what my Father has commanded me. "Come now; let us leave. *(the prince of this world)

40. DON'T <u>WORRY</u>

Mt 6:25	"Therefore I tell you, do not worry about your life, what you will eat or drink; or about your body, what you will wear. Is not life more than food, and the body more than clothes?
Mt 6:28	"And why do you worry about clothes? See how the flowers of the field grow. They do not labor or spin.
Mt 6:31	So do not worry, saying, 'What shall we eat?' or 'What shall we drink?' or 'What shall we wear?'
Mt 6:34	Therefore do not worry about tomorrow, for tomorrow will worry about itself. Each day has enough trouble of its own.
Mt 10:19	But when they arrest you, do not worry about what to say or how to say it. At that time you will be given what to say,
Mt 13:22	The seed falling among the thorns refers to someone who hears the word, but the worries of this life and the deceitfulness of wealth choke the word, making it unfruitful.
Mk 4:18	Still others, like seed sown among thorns, hear the word; [...]
Mk 4:19	[...] but the worries of this life, the deceitfulness of wealth and the desires for other things come in and choke the word, making it unfruitful.

Mk 13:11	Whenever you are arrested and brought to trial, do not worry beforehand about what to say. Just say whatever is given you at the time, for it is not you speaking, but the Holy Spirit.
Lk 10:39	She* had a sister called Mary, who sat at the Lord's feet listening to what he said. *(Martha) [...]
Lk 10:40	[...] But Martha was distracted by all the preparations that had to be made. She came to him and asked, "Lord, don't you care that my sister has left me to do the work by myself? Tell her to help me!" [...]
Lk 10:41	[...] "Martha, Martha," the Lord answered, "you are worried and upset about many things, [...]
Lk 10:42	[...] but few things are needed—or indeed only one. Mary has chosen what is better, and it will not be taken away from her."
Lk 12:11	"When you are brought before synagogues, rulers and authorities, do not worry about how you will defend yourselves or what you will say, [...]
Lk 12:12	[...] for the Holy Spirit will teach you at that time what you should say."
Lk 12:22	Then Jesus said to his disciples: "Therefore I tell you, do not worry about your life, what you will eat; or about your body, what you will wear.
Lk 12:25	Who of you by worrying can add a single hour to your life? [...]
Lk 12:26	[...] Since you cannot do this very little thing, why do you worry about the rest?

Lk 12:29	And do not set your heart on what you will eat or drink; do not worry about it.
Lk 21:14	But* make up your mind not to worry beforehand how you will defend yourselves. *(when you are seized during end times) [...]
Lk 21:15	[...] For I will give you words and wisdom that none of your adversaries will be able to resist or contradict.
Lk 21:34	"Be careful, or your hearts will be weighed down with carousing, drunkenness and the anxieties of life, and that day will close on you suddenly like a trap. [...]
Lk 21:35	[...] For it will come on all those who live on the face of the whole earth.
Lk 24:36	While they* were still talking about this,** Jesus himself stood among them*** and said to them, "Peace be with you." *(two travelers) **(that Jesus was risen and earlier was recognized by some of them) ***(the eleven and those with them) [...]
Lk 24:38	[...] He said to them,* "Why are you troubled, and why do doubts rise in your minds? *(the eleven and those with them)
Jn 14:1	"Do not let your hearts be troubled. You believe in God; believe also in me.
Jn 14:27	Peace I leave with you; my peace I give you. I do not give to you as the world gives. Do not let your hearts be troubled and do not be afraid.

Jn 16:33   "I have told you these things,* so that in me
           you may have peace. In this world you will
           have trouble. But take heart! I have overcome
           the world." *(the disciples will be scattered
           and the Father is with Jesus)

APPENDIX

APPENDIX A

AN ANNOTATED CONCORDANCE
OF THE GOSPELS
FOR
GOD'S TEN COMMANDMENTS
FOUND IN
EXODUS 20:2-17 and DEUTERONOMY 5:6-21

1. You shall have no other gods before me.
2. You shall not make or bow down to an image.
3. You shall not misuse the name of the Lord your God.
4. Remember the Sabbath day by keeping it holy.
5. Honor your father and your mother.
6. You shall not murder.
7. You shall not commit adultery.
8. You shall not steal.
9. You shall not give false testimony against your neighbor.
10. You shall not covet anything of your neighbors

1. YOU SHALL HAVE NO OTHER GODS BEFORE ME

Mt 4:10 — Jesus said to him, "Away from me, Satan! For it is written: 'Worship the Lord your God, and serve him only.'"

Mt 6:24 — "No one can serve two masters. Either you will hate the one and love the other, or you will be devoted to the one and despise the other. You cannot serve both God and money.

Mt 6:33 — But seek first his kingdom and his righteousness, and all these things will be given to you as well.

Mt 22:37 — Jesus replied:* "'Love the Lord your God with all your heart and with all your soul and with all your mind. *(to the expert in the law) [...]

Mt 22:38 — [...] This is the first and greatest commandment. [...]

Mt 22:39 — [...] And the second is like it: 'Love your neighbor as yourself.' [...]

Mt 22:40 — [...] All the Law and the Prophets hang on these two commandments."

Mt 23:9 — And do not call anyone on earth 'father,' for you have one Father, and he is in heaven.

Mt 23:23   "Woe to you, teachers of the law and Pharisees, you hypocrites! You give a tenth of your spices—mint, dill and cumin. But you have neglected the more important matters of the law—justice, mercy and faithfulness. You should have practiced the latter, without neglecting the former.

Mk 12:29   "The most important one,"* answered Jesus,** "is this: 'Hear, O Israel: The Lord our God, the Lord is one. *(commandment) **(to a teacher of the law) [...]

Mk 12:30   [...] Love the Lord your God with all your heart and with all your soul and with all your mind and with all your strength.' [...]

Mk 12:31   [...] The second is this: 'Love your neighbor as yourself.' There is no commandment greater than these." [...]

Mk 12:32   [...] "Well said, teacher," the man replied. "You are right in saying that God is one and there is no other but him. [...]

Mk 12:33   […] To love him* with all your heart, with all your understanding and with all your strength, and to love your neighbor as yourself is more important than all burnt offerings and sacrifices." *(God) […]

Mk 12:34   [...] When Jesus saw that he* had answered wisely, he said to him, "You are not far from the kingdom of God." And from then on no one dared ask him any more questions. *(a teacher of the law)

Lk 4:8   Jesus answered,* "It is written: 'Worship the Lord your God and serve him only.'" *(to the devil)

Lk 10:27   He* answered, "'Love the Lord your God with all your heart and with all your soul and with all your strength and with all your mind'; and, 'Love your neighbor as yourself.'" *(an expert in the law who asked how to inherit eternal life) [...]

Lk 10:28   [...] "You have answered correctly," Jesus replied. "Do this and you will live."

Lk 11:42   "Woe to you Pharisees, because you give God a tenth of your mint, rue and all other kinds of garden herbs, but you neglect justice and the love of God. You should have practiced the latter without leaving the former undone.

Lk 12:21   "This* is how it will be with whoever stores up things for themselves but is not rich toward God." *(like a dying man who cannot take his possessions with him)

Lk 12:31   But seek his kingdom, and these things will be given to you as well.

Lk 16:13   "No one can serve two masters. Either you will hate the one and love the other, or you will be devoted to the one and despise the other. You cannot serve both God and money."

2. YOU SHALL NOT MAKE OR BOW DOWN TO AN IMAGE

(No verses in the Gospels)

3. YOU SHALL NOT MISUSE THE NAME OF THE LORD YOUR GOD

(No verses in the Gospels. Also see #7 Don't Blaspheme against Holy Spirit.)

4. REMEMBER THE SABBATH DAY BY KEEPING IT HOLY

Mt 12:12	How much more valuable is a person than a sheep! Therefore it is lawful to do good on the Sabbath." [...]
Mt 12:13	[...] then he said to the man, "Stretch out your hand." So he stretched it out and it was completely restored, just as sound as the other.
Mk 1:21	They* went to Capernaum, and when the Sabbath came, Jesus went into the synagogue and began to teach. *(Jesus and his followers)
Mk 2:27	Then he said to them,* "The Sabbath was made for man, not man for the Sabbath. *(the Pharisees) [...]
Mk 2:28	[...] So the Son of Man is Lord even of the Sabbath."
Mk 3:4	Then Jesus asked them,* "Which is lawful on the Sabbath: to do good or to do evil, to save life or to kill?" But they remained silent. *(the Pharisees) [...]
Mk 3:5	[...] He looked around at them* in anger and, deeply distressed at their stubborn hearts, said to the man, "Stretch out your hand." He stretched it out, and his hand was completely restored. *(the Pharisees)

Mk 6:2	When the Sabbath came, he began to teach in the synagogue, and many who heard him were amazed. "Where did this man get these things?" they asked. "What's this wisdom that has been given him? What are these remarkable miracles he is performing?
Lk 4:31	Then he went down to Capernaum, a town in Galilee, and on the Sabbath he taught the people.
Lk 6:5	Then Jesus said to them,* "The Son of Man is Lord of the Sabbath." *(the Pharisees)
Lk 6:6	On another Sabbath he went into the synagogue and was teaching, and a man was there whose right hand was shriveled. [...]
Lk 6:9	[...] Then Jesus said to them,* "I ask you, which is lawful on the Sabbath: to do good or to do evil, to save life or to destroy it?" *(the Pharisees and the teachers of the law) [...]
Lk 6:10	[...] He looked around at them all, and then said to the man, "Stretch out your hand." He did so, and his hand was completely restored.
Lk 13:10	On a Sabbath Jesus was teaching in one of the synagogues,
Lk 13:13	Then he* put his hands on her,** and immediately she straightened up and praised God. *(Jesus cured on the Sabbath) **(a crippled woman)
Lk 14:3	Jesus asked the Pharisees and experts in the law, "Is it lawful to heal on the Sabbath or not?" [...]

Lk 14:4	[...] But they remained silent. So taking hold of the man, he healed him and sent him on his way.
Jn 5:9	At once the man was cured; he picked up his mat and walked. The day on which this took place was a Sabbath,
Jn 9:14	Now the day on which Jesus had made the mud and opened the man's eyes was a Sabbath.

5. HONOR YOUR FATHER AND YOUR MOTHER

Mt 15:4   For God said, 'Honor your father and mother'
           and 'Anyone who curses their father or mother
           is to be put to death.'

Mt 19:19   honor your father and mother,' and 'love your
           neighbor as yourself.'"

Mk 7:10   For Moses said, 'Honor your father and
           mother,' and, 'Anyone who curses their father
           or mother is to be put to death.'

Mk 10:19   You know the commandments: 'You shall
           not murder, you shall not commit adultery,
           you shall not steal, you shall not give false
           testimony, you shall not defraud, honor your
           father and mother.'"

Lk 18:20   You know the commandments: 'You shall
           not commit adultery, you shall not murder,
           you shall not steal, you shall not give false
           testimony, honor your father and mother.'"

6. YOU SHALL NOT MURDER

Mt 5:21   "You have heard that it was said to the people long ago, 'You shall not murder, and anyone who murders will be subject to judgment.'

Mt 15:19   For out of the heart come evil thoughts—murder, adultery, sexual immorality, theft, false testimony, slander [...]

Mt 15:20   [...] These* are what defile a person; but eating with unwashed hands does not defile them." *(Mt 15:19)

Mt 19:18   "Which ones?"* he** inquired. Jesus replied, "'You shall not murder, you shall not commit adultery, you shall not steal, you shall not give false testimony, *(commandments needed for eternal life) **(a man)

Mk 7:21   For it is from within, out of a person's heart, that evil thoughts come—sexual immorality, theft, murder, [...]

Mk 7:22   [...] adultery, greed, malice, deceit, lewdness, envy, slander, arrogance and folly. [...]

Mk 7:23   [...] All these* evils come from inside and defile a person." *(Mk 7:21 and Mk 7:22)

Mk 10:19   You know the commandments: 'You shall not murder, you shall not commit adultery, you shall not steal, you shall not give false testimony, you shall not defraud, honor your father and mother.'"

Lk 18:20   You know the commandments: 'You shall
            not commit adultery, you shall not murder,
            you shall not steal, you shall not give false
            testimony, honor your father and mother.'"

7. YOU SHALL NOT COMMIT ADULTERY

Mt 5:27	"You have heard that it was said, 'You shall not commit adultery.' [...]
Mt 5:28	[...] But I tell you that anyone who looks at a woman lustfully has already committed adultery with her in his heart.
Mt 5:32	But I tell you that anyone who divorces his wife, except for sexual immorality, makes her the victim of adultery, and anyone who marries a divorced woman commits adultery.
Mt 15:19	For out of the heart come evil thoughts— murder, adultery, sexual immorality, theft, false testimony, slander. [...]
Mt 15:20	[...] These* are what defile a person; but eating with unwashed hands does not defile them." *(Mt 15:19)
Mt 19:9	I tell you that anyone who divorces his wife, except for sexual immorality, and marries another woman commits adultery."
Mt 19:18	"Which ones?"* he** inquired. Jesus replied, "'You shall not murder, you shall not commit adultery, you shall not steal, you shall not give false testimony, *(commandments needed for eternal life) **(a man)
Mk 7:21	For it is from within, out of a person's heart, that evil thoughts come—sexual immorality, theft, murder, [...]

Mk 7:22	[...] adultery, greed, malice, deceit, lewdness, envy, slander, arrogance and folly. [...]
Mk 7:23	[...] All these* evils come from inside and defile a person." *(Mk 7:21 and Mk 7:22)
Mk 10:11	He answered, "Anyone who divorces his wife and marries another woman commits adultery against her. [...]
Mk 10:12	[...] And if she* divorces her husband and marries another man, she commits adultery." *(a wife)
Mk 10:19	You know the commandments: 'You shall not murder, you shall not commit adultery, you shall not steal, you shall not give false testimony, you shall not defraud, honor your father and mother.'"
Lk 16:18	"Anyone who divorces his wife and marries another woman commits adultery, and the man who marries a divorced woman commits adultery.
Lk 18:20	You know the commandments: 'You shall not commit adultery, you shall not murder, you shall not steal, you shall not give false testimony, honor your father and mother.'"
Jn 8:7	When they* kept on questioning him, he straightened up and said to them, "Let any one of you who is without sin be the first to throw a stone at her."** *(the teachers of the law and the Pharisees) **(a woman caught in the act of adultery) [...]
Jn 8:10	[...] Jesus straightened up and asked her, "Woman, where are they? Has no one condemned you?" [...]

Jn 8:11   [...] "No one, sir," she* said. "Then neither do
            I condemn you," Jesus declared. "Go now and
            leave your life of sin." *(the woman caught in
            the act of adultery)

8. YOU SHALL NOT STEAL

Mt 15:19　For out of the heart come evil thoughts—murder, adultery, sexual immorality, theft, false testimony, slander. [...]

Mt 15:20　[...] These* are what defile a person; but eating with unwashed hands does not defile them." *(Mt 15:19)

Mt 19:18　"Which ones?"* he** inquired. Jesus replied, "'You shall not murder, you shall not commit adultery, you shall not steal, you shall not give false testimony, *(commandments needed for eternal life) **(a man)

Mk 7:21　For it is from within, out of a person's heart, that evil thoughts come—sexual immorality, theft, murder, [...]

Mk 7:22　[...] adultery, greed, malice, deceit, lewdness, envy, slander, arrogance and folly. [...]

Mk 7:23　[...] All these* evils come from inside and defile a person." *(Mk 7:21 and Mk 7:22)

Mk 10:19　You know the commandments: 'You shall not murder, you shall not commit adultery, you shall not steal, you shall not give false testimony, you shall not defraud, honor your father and mother.'"

Lk 18:20　You know the commandments: 'You shall not commit adultery, you shall not murder, you shall not steal, you shall not give false testimony, honor your father and mother.'"

9. YOU SHALL NOT BEAR FALSE WITNESS AGAINST YOUR NEIGHBOR

Mt 15:19	For out of the heart come evil thoughts—murder, adultery, sexual immorality, theft, false testimony, slander. [...]
Mt 15:20	[...] These* are what defile a person; but eating with unwashed hands does not defile them." *(Mt 15:19)
Mt 19:18	"Which ones?"* he** inquired. Jesus replied, "'You shall not murder, you shall not commit adultery, you shall not steal, you shall not give false testimony, *(commandments needed for eternal life) **(a man)
Mk 7:21	For it is from within, out of a person's heart, that evil thoughts come—sexual immorality, theft, murder, [...]
Mk 7:22	[...] adultery, greed, malice, deceit, lewdness, envy, slander, arrogance and folly. [...]
Mk 7:23	[...] All these* evils come from inside and defile a person." *(Mk 7:21 and Mk 7:22)
Mk 10:19	You know the commandments: 'You shall not murder, you shall not commit adultery, you shall not steal, you shall not give false testimony, you shall not defraud, honor your father and mother.'"
Lk 18:20	You know the commandments: 'You shall not commit adultery, you shall not murder, you shall not steal, you shall not give false testimony, honor your father and mother.'"

10. YOU SHALL NOT COVET ANYTHING
OF YOUR NEIGHBORS

Mk 7:21   For it is from within, out of a person's heart,
           that evil thoughts come—sexual immorality,
           theft, murder, [...]

Mk 7:22   [...] adultery, greed, malice, deceit, lewdness,
           envy, slander, arrogance and folly. [...]

Mk 7:23   [...] All these* evils come from inside and
           defile a person." *(Mk 7:21 and Mk 7:22)

APPENDIX B

THE LORD'S PRAYER

Mt 6:9	"This, then, is how you should pray: "'Our Father in heaven, hallowed be your name,
Mt 6:10	your kingdom come, your will be done, on earth as it is in heaven.
Mt 6:11	Give us today our daily bread.
Mt 6:12	And forgive us our debts, as we also have forgiven our debtors.
Mt 6:13	And lead us not into temptation, but deliver us from the evil one.'
Lk 11:2	He said to them,* "When you pray, say: "'Father, hallowed be your name, your kingdom come. *(the disciples)
Lk 11:3	Give us each day our daily bread.
Lk 11:4	Forgive us our sins, for we also forgive everyone who sins against us. And lead us not into temptation.

APPENDIX C

INSTRUCTIONS FOR DISCIPLES

Mt 10:5   These twelve Jesus sent out with the following instructions: "Do not go among the Gentiles or enter any town of the Samaritans.

Mt 10:6   Go rather to the lost sheep of Israel.

Mt 10:7   As you go, proclaim this message: 'The kingdom of heaven has come near.'

Mt 10:8   Heal the sick, raise the dead, cleanse those who have leprosy, drive out demons. Freely you have received; freely give.

Mt 10:9   "Do not get any gold or silver or copper to take with you in your belts- [...]

Mt 10:10   [...] no bag for the journey or extra shirt or sandals or a staff, for the worker is worth his keep.

Mt 10:11   Whatever town or village you enter, search there for some worthy person and stay at their house until you leave.

Mt 10:12   As you enter the home, give it your greeting.

Mt 10:13   If the home is deserving, let your peace rest on it; if it is not, let your peace return to you.

Mt 10:14	If anyone will not welcome you or listen to your words, leave that home or town and shake the dust off your feet.
Mt 10:16	"I am sending you out like sheep among wolves. Therefore be as shrewd as snakes and as innocent as doves.
Mt 10:17	Be on your guard; you will be handed over to the local councils and be flogged in the synagogues.
Mt 10:19	But when they arrest you, do not worry about what to say or how to say it. At that time you will be given what to say,
Mt 10:22	You will be hated by everyone because of me, but the one who stands firm to the end will be saved.
Mt 10:23	When you are persecuted in one place, flee to another. Truly I tell you, you will not finish going through the towns of Israel before the Son of Man comes.
Mt 10:26	"So do not be afraid of them,* for there is nothing concealed that will not be disclosed, or hidden that will not be made known. *(those of the house of Beelzebul)
Mt 10:27	What I tell you in the dark, speak in the daylight; what is whispered in your ear, proclaim from the roofs.
Mt 10:28	Do not be afraid of those who kill the body but cannot kill the soul. Rather, be afraid of the One who can destroy both soul and body in hell.
Mt 10:31	So don't be afraid; you are worth more than many sparrows.

Mt 16:19	I will give you* the keys of the kingdom of heaven; whatever you bind on earth will be bound in heaven, and whatever you loose on earth will be loosed in heaven." *(Peter)
Mt 28:19	Therefore go and make disciples of all nations, baptizing them in the name of the Father and of the Son and of the Holy Spirit, [...]
Mt 28:20	[...] and teaching them* to obey everything I have commanded you. And surely I am with you always, to the very end of the age." *(disciples of all nations)
Mk 6:7	Calling the Twelve to him, he began to send them out two by two and gave them authority over impure spirits.
Mk 6:8	These were his instructions: "Take nothing for the journey except a staff—no bread, no bag, no money in your belts.
Mk 6:9	Wear sandals but not an extra shirt.
Mk 6:10	Whenever you enter a house, stay there until you leave that town.
Mk 6:11	And if any place will not welcome you or listen to you, leave that place and shake the dust off your feet as a testimony against them."
Lk 9:1	When Jesus had called the Twelve together, he gave them power and authority to drive out all demons and to cure diseases,
Lk 9:2	and he sent them* out to proclaim the kingdom of God and to heal the sick. *(the twelve)
Lk 9:3	He told them: "Take nothing for the journey— no staff, no bag, no bread, no money, no extra shirt.

Lk 9:4	Whatever house you enter, stay there until you leave that town.
Lk 9:5	If people do not welcome you, leave their town and shake the dust off your feet as a testimony against them."
Lk 10:1	After this the Lord appointed seventy-two others and sent them two by two ahead of him to every town and place where he was about to go. [...]
Lk 10:2	[...] He told them,* "The harvest is plentiful, but the workers are few. Ask the Lord of the harvest, therefore, to send out workers into his harvest field. *(the seventy-two appointed to proceed him)
Lk 10:3	Go! I am sending you out like lambs among wolves.
Lk 10:4	Do not take a purse or bag or sandals; and do not greet anyone on the road.
Lk 10:5	"When you enter a house, first say, 'Peace to this house.'
Lk 10:7	Stay there, eating and drinking whatever they give you, for the worker deserves his wages. Do not move around from house to house.
Lk 10:8	"When you enter a town and are welcomed, eat what is offered to you.
Lk 10:9	Heal the sick who are there and tell them, 'The kingdom of God has come near to you.'
Lk 10:10	But when you enter a town and are not welcomed, go into its streets and say, [...]
Lk 10:11	[...] 'Even the dust of your town we wipe from our feet as a warning to you. Yet be sure of this: The kingdom of God has come near.' [...]

Lk 10:12 [...] I tell you, it will be more bearable on that day for Sodom than for that town.

Lk 22:36 He said to them, "But now* if you have a purse, take it, and also a bag; and if you don't have a sword, sell your cloak and buy one. *(just before death of Jesus)

Jn 21:15 When they had finished eating, Jesus said to Simon Peter, "Simon son of John, do you love me more than these?" "Yes, Lord," he said, "you know that I love you." Jesus said, "Feed my lambs."

Jn 21:16 Again Jesus said, "Simon son of John, do you love me?" He answered, "Yes, Lord, you know that I love you." Jesus said, "Take care of my sheep."

Jn 21:17 The third time he said to him, "Simon son of John, do you love me?" Peter was hurt because Jesus asked him a third time, "Do you love me?" He said, "Lord, you know all things; you know that I love you." Jesus said, "Feed my sheep.

APPENDIX D

BLESSED (BEATITUDES)

Mt 5:3	"Blessed are the poor in spirit, for theirs is the kingdom of heaven.
Mt 5:4	Blessed are those who mourn, for they will be conforted.
Mt 5:5	Blessed are the meek, for they will inherit the earth.
Mt 5:6	Blessed are those who hunger and thirst for righteousness, for they will be filled.
Mt 5:7	Blessed are the merciful, for they will be shown mercy.
Mt 5:8	Blessed are the pure in heart, for they will see God.
Mt 5:9	Blessed are the peacemakers, for they will be called children of God.
Mt 5:10	Blessed are those who are persecuted because of righteousness, for theirs is the kingdom of heaven.
Mt 5:11	"Blessed are you when people insult you, persecute you and falsely say all kinds of evil against you because of me. [...]

Mt 5:12	[...] Rejoice and be glad, because great is your reward in heaven, for in the same way they persecuted the prophets who were before you.
Mt 11:6	Blessed is anyone who does not stumble on account of me."
Mt 13:16	But blessed are your eyes because they see, and your ears because they hear.
Mt 24:46	It will be good* for that servant whose master finds him doing so** when he returns. *(blessed) **(being faithful)
Lk 1:48	for he* has been mindful of the humble state of his servant. From now on all generations will call me** blessed, *(God) **(Mary)
Lk 6:20	Looking at his disciples, he said: "Blessed are you who are poor, for yours is the kingdom of God.
Lk 6:21	Blessed are you who hunger now, for you will be satisfied. Blessed are you who weep now, for you will laugh.
Lk 6:22	Blessed are you when people hate you, when they exclude you and insult you and reject your name as evil, because of the Son of Man. [...]
Lk 6:23	[...] "Rejoice in that day and leap for joy, because great is your reward in heaven. For that is how their ancestors treated the prophets.
Lk 7:23	Blessed is anyone who does not stumble on account of me."
Lk 10:23	Then he turned to his disciples and said privately, "Blessed are the eyes that see what you see.

Lk 11:27	As Jesus was saying these things, a woman in the crowd called out, "Blessed is the mother who gave you birth and nursed you." [...]
Lk 11:28	[...] He replied, "Blessed rather are those who hear the word of God and obey it."
Lk 12:37	It will be good* for those servants whose master finds them watching when he comes. Truly I tell you, he will dress himself to serve, will have them recline at the table and will come and wait on them. *(blessed) [...]
Lk 12:38	[...] It will be good* for those servants whose master finds them ready, even if he comes in the middle of the night or toward daybreak. *(blessed)
Lk 12:43	It will be good* for that servant whom the master finds doing so** when he returns. *(blessed) **(being faithful)
Lk 14:13	But when you give a banquet, invite the poor, the crippled, the lame, the blind, [...]
Lk 14:14	[...] and you will be blessed. Although they cannot repay you, you will be repaid at the resurrection of the righteous."
Lk 19:38	"Blessed is the king who comes in the name of the Lord!" "Peace in heaven and glory in the highest!"
Lk 23:29	For the time will come when you will say, 'Blessed are the childless women, the wombs that never bore and the breasts that never nursed!'
Jn 13:16	Very truly I tell you, no servant is greater than his master, nor is a messenger greater than the one who sent him. [...]

Jn 13:17   [...] Now that you know these things* you will
              be blessed if you do them. *(Jesus examples)

Jn 20:29   Then Jesus told him,* "Because you have
              seen me, you have believed; blessed are those
              who have not seen and yet have believed."
              *(Thomas)

APPENDIX E

WOES

Mt 11:21   "Woe to you, Chorazin! Woe to you, Bethsaida! For if the miracles that were performed in you had been performed in Tyre and Sidon, they would have repented long ago in sackcloth and ashes.

Mt 18:7   Woe to the world because of the things that cause people to stumble! Such things must come, but woe to the person through whom they come!

Mt 23:13   "Woe to you, teachers of the law and Pharisees, you hypocrites! You shut the door of the kingdom of heaven in people's faces. You yourselves do not enter, nor will you let those enter who are trying to.

Mt 23:15   "Woe to you, teachers of the law and Pharisees, you hypocrites! You travel over land and sea to win a single convert, and when you have succeeded, you make them twice as much a child of hell as you are.

Mt 23:16	"Woe to you, blind guides! You say, 'If anyone swears by the temple, it means nothing; but anyone who swears by the gold of the temple is bound by that oath.'
Mt 23:23	"Woe to you, teachers of the law and Pharisees, you hypocrites! You give a tenth of your spices—mint, dill and cumin. But you have neglected the more important matters of the law—justice, mercy and faithfulness. You should have practiced the latter, without neglecting the former.
Mt 23:25	"Woe to you, teachers of the law and Pharisees, you hypocrites! You clean the outside of the cup and dish, but inside they are full of greed and self-indulgence.
Mt 23:27	"Woe to you, teachers of the law and Pharisees, you hypocrites! You are like whitewashed tombs, which look beautiful on the outside but on the inside are full of the bones of the dead and everything unclean.
Mt 23:29	"Woe to you, teachers of the law and Pharisees, you hypocrites! You build tombs for the prophets and decorate the graves of the righteous.
Mt 24:19	How dreadful* it will be in those** days for pregnant women and nursing mothers! *(woe) **(end) [same wording as Mk 13:17]
Mt 26:24	The Son of Man will go just as it is written about him. But woe to that man who betrays the Son of Man! It would be better for him if he had not been born." [same wording as Mk 14:21]

Mk 13:17	How dreadful* it will be in those** days for pregnant women and nursing mothers! *(woe) **(end) [same wording as Mt 24:19]
Mk 14:21	The Son of Man will go just as it is written about him. But woe to that man who betrays the Son of Man! It would be better for him if he had not been born." [same wording as Mt 26:24]
Lk 6:24	"But woe to you who are rich, for you have already received your comfort.
Lk 6:25	Woe to you who are well fed now, for you will go hungry. Woe to you who laugh now, for you will mourn and weep.
Lk 6:26	Woe to you when everyone speaks well of you, for that is how their ancestors treated the false prophets.
Lk 10:13	"Woe to you, Chorazin! Woe to you, Bethsaida! For if the miracles that were performed in you had been performed in Tyre and Sidon, they would have repented long ago, sitting in sackcloth and ashes.
Lk 11:42	"Woe to you Pharisees, because you give God a tenth of your mint, rue and all other kinds of garden herbs, but you neglect justice and the love of God. You should have practiced the latter without leaving the former undone.
Lk 11:43	"Woe to you Pharisees, because you love the most important seats in the synagogues and respectful greetings in the marketplaces.
Lk 11:44	"Woe to you, because you are like unmarked graves, which people walk over without knowing it."

Lk 11:46	Jesus replied, "And you experts in the law, woe to you, because you load people down with burdens they can hardly carry, and you yourselves will not lift one finger to help them.
Lk 11:47	"Woe to you, because you build tombs for the prophets, and it was your ancestors who killed them.
Lk 11:52	"Woe to you experts in the law, because you have taken away the key to knowledge. You yourselves have not entered, and you have hindered those who were entering."
Lk 17:1	Jesus said to his disciples: "Things that cause people to stumbles are bound to come, but woe to anyone through whom they come.
Lk 21:23	How dreadful* it will be in those** days for pregnant women and nursing mothers! There will be great distress in the land and wrath against this people. *(woe) **(end)
Lk 22:22	The Son of Man will go as it has been decreed. But woe to that man who betrays him!"

APPENDIX F

PARABLES & LESSONS

Mt 13:1-9	**Sower** spreads seed on rich soil and produces fruit
Mt 13:18-23	**Sower** parable explanation
Mt 13:24-30	**Weeds** sowed among wheat to be separated later
Mt 13:31-32	Kingdom of heaven like **mustard seed** which grows large
Mt 13:33	Kingdom of heaven like **yeast** in flour which leavens entire batch
Mt 13:36-43	**Weeds** parable explanation
Mt 13:44	Kingdom like **treasure** in a field
Mt 13:45-46	Kingdom like a fine **pearl**
Mt 13:47-50	Kingdom like **net** thrown into the sea which catches good and bad
Mt 13:52	Kingdom like **homeowner** with valuables
Mt 18:12-14	Rejoicing over one **lost sheep**
Mt 18:23-35	**King has compassion** on servant who in turn has no pity
Mt 20:1-16	Kingdom like landowner who pays all **workers same wages**

Mt 21:28-32	One **son** who works in field and one son who does not
Mt 21:33-45	**Tenants of vineyard are replaced** after killing landowner's servants and son
Mt 22:1-14	**Wedding feast** where good and bad are invited
Mt 22:15-22	Paying **taxes**
Mt 22:23-33	**Marriage at the resurrection**
Mt 23:1-12	Warning against **hypocrisy**
Mt 24:32-35	Lesson of **fig tree** / leaves indicate summer is near like end times
Mt 24:45-51	Lesson of **faithful and unfaithful servant** – each receives justice
Mt 25:1-13	**Ten virgins** – five prepared with lamps and five without
Mt 25:14-30	**Bags of God** – two servants make profit for master and one does not
Mt 25:31-46	People will be separated like **sheep from goats**
Mk 2:21	Never patch **old garment** with new material
Mk 2:22	Never pour new wine in **old wineskins**
Mk 3:23-27	**Satan** cannot drive out Satan
Mk 4:2-9	**Sower** spreads seed on rich soil and produces fruit
Mk 4:14-20	**Sower** parable explained
Mk 4:21-22	Lamp should be placed on a **lampstand**
Mk 4:26-29	Kingdom like man who **scattered seed**
Mk 4:30-32	Kingdom of heaven like **mustard seed** which grows large
Mk 7:1-23	Lesson of **unclean hands** – foods and hands don't defile
Mk 12:1-11	**Tenants of vineyard are replaced** after killing landowner's servants and son

Mk 13:28-31	Lesson of **fig tree** / leaves indicate summer is near like end times
Mk 13:32-37	The **end day** is unknown
Lk 5:36	Don't patch **old garment** with new material
Lk 5:37-39	Don't pour new wine in **old wineskins**
Lk 6:39-40	**Blind** cannot lead blind
Lk 6:43-45	Tree known by **fruit** like individuals known by their speech
Lk 6:47-49	To listen and act is like a **house** with foundation
Lk 7:41-43	One who owes **500 denarii** another who owes 50 to money lenders
Lk 8:4-15	**Sower** spreads seed on rich soil and produces fruit
Lk 8:16-18	Lamp should be placed on a **lampstand**
Lk 10:30-37	**Good Samaritan** helps man hurt by robbers
Lk 11:5-13	**Neighbor gives** loaves of bread when asked
Lk 11:17-20	House **divided** will fall – also if Satan divided
Lk 11:21-22	**Strong man guards house** until stronger man comes
Lk 11:24-26	**Impure spirit returns** with more wicked spirits
Lk 11:29-32	Someone greater than **Solomon and Jonah** is here
Lk 11:33-36	Simile – lamp on lampstand / **lamp of body** is eye
Lk 12:16-21	Rich fool decides to build **larger barn** to hold harvest
Lk 12:35-48	**Faithful servants** are ready when unexpected master comes
Lk 12:51-53	Jesus came not for peace but for **division**
Lk 13:6-9	**Barren fig tree** is nurtured

Lk 13:18-19	Kingdom of heaven is like **mustard seed** which grows large
Lk 13:20-21	Kingdom of heaven like **yeast** in flour which leavens entire batch
Lk 14:7-11	Front **seats at wedding** are not to be chosen first
Lk 14:12-14	**Invite** those who cannot repay you
Lk 14:16-24	Great **dinner** to which many are invited
Lk 14:28-33	Plan before **building tower** or going to war
Lk 14:34-35	Simile of **salt** – not good if looses its taste
Lk 15:3-7	Rejoicing over **one lost sheep** which is found
Lk 15:8-10	Rejoicing over **one lost coin** which is found
Lk 15:11-32	Rejoicing over **one lost son** who returns
Lk 16:1-15	Actions of **shrewd manager**
Lk 16:19-31	Afterlife of rich man verses **afterlife of Lazarus**
Lk 18:1-8	**Persistent widow** granted justice by judge
Lk 18:9-14	Prayer of Pharisee verses prayer of **tax collector**
Lk 19:1-10	**Tax collector** Zacchaeus changes lifestyle
Lk 19:11-27	**Ten gold coins** given by nobleman to be engaged in trade
Lk 20:9-18	**Tenants of vineyard are replaced** after killing landowner's servants and son
Lk 20:27-38	**Resurrection and Marriage**
Lk 21:29-33	**Fig tree buds** tell summer is near like signs tell when kingdom is near
Jn 3:1-18	To enter the kingdom of God you must be **born again**
Jn 3:19-21	**Live by truth**, come into light
Jn 5:36-47	**Testimonies** about Jesus
Jn 10:1-18	Jesus is **good shepherd**

Jn 14:5-12	**Way to Father**
Jn 14:16-17	Promise of **Holy Spirit**
Jn 15:1-8	Jesus is **vine and branches**
Jn 16:21-22	Like **woman in labor**, grief now and rejoice later

NOTE: For lessons regarding approval of curing on the Sabbath, see Appendix A #4.

APPENDIX G

MIRACLES

Mt 4:23-24	All with various diseases
Mt 8:2-4	Leper
Mt 8:5-13	Paralyzed centurion's servant
Mt 8:14-15	Fever in Simon Peter's mother-in-law
Mt 8:16	Many possessed and sick
Mt 8:23-27	Wind calmed
Mt 8:28-34	Two demons go into pigs
Mt 9:1-8	Paralytic (and sins)
Mt 9:18-19&9:23-26	Officials daughter brought to life
Mt 9:20-22	Hemorrhage in woman
Mt 9:27-31	Two blind men
Mt 9:32-33	Mute and demon possessed man
Mt 9:35	Every disease and sickness
Mt 12:9-13	Withered hand on Sabbath
Mt 12:15	Cured all ill following Jesus
Mt 12:22-23	Mute, blind and demon possessed man
Mt 13:54-58	Cured only a few in Nazareth because lack of faith
Mt 14:14	Sick in the large crowd
Mt 14:15-21	Fed 5000 plus women and children
Mt 14:22-27	Jesus walks on water

Mt 14:28-33	Peter walks on water but fears
Mt 14:34-36	Many sick touched his cloak
Mt 15:21-28	Demon in Canaanite woman's daughter
Mt 15:29-31	Lame, blind, crippled, mute and others
Mt 15:32-38	Fed 4000 plus women and children
Mt 17:1-7	Jesus is transfigured / God speaks – pleased with Son – Listen to him!
Mt 17:14-21	Needed faith to heal son with demon
Mt 19:1-2	Cured all in large crowds
Mt 20:29-34	Two blind men
Mt 21:14	Blind and lame in temple
Mt 21:18-19	Jesus withered a fig tree
Mk 1:11	God speaks – pleased with one He loves
Mk 1:23-28	Unclean spirit
Mk 1:29-31	Fever in Simon Peter's mother-in-law
Mk 1:32-34	Various diseases and those possessed by demons
Mk 1:39	Demons
Mk 1:40-45	Leper
Mk 2:1-12	Paralytic brought thru roof
Mk 3:1-5	Withered hand on the Sabbath
Mk 3:10	Those with diseases touched Jesus
Mk 4:35-41	Calmed storm
Mk 5:1-20	Many demons go out of man and into pigs
Mk 5:22-23&5:35-43	Jairus' daughter brought to life
Mk 5:24-34	Hemorrhage in woman
Mk 6:4-6	Cured only a few in his hometown because lack of faith
Mk 6:13	[The twelve drove out demons and cured sick]
Mk 6:35-44	Fed 5000 men with 5 loaves and 2 fish

Mk 6:45-51	Walked on water
Mk 6:53-56	Many sick touched his cloak
Mk 7:24-30	Demons in Syrophoenician woman's daughter
Mk 7:31-37	Deaf man who could hardly speak
Mk 8:1-9	Fed 4000 with 7 loaves and a few fish
Mk 8:22-26	Blind man in Bethsaida
Mk 9:2-10	Jesus is transfigured / God speaks – love of Son – Listen to him!
Mk 9:14-29	Boy with impure spirit cured by prayer
Mk 10:46-52	Blind Bartimaeus
Mk 11:12-14&20-21	Withered a fig tree
Mk 16:9	Jesus rose / also 7 demons from Mary Magdalene
Lk 3:21-22	God speaks – pleased with Son He loves
Lk 4:33-37	Demon in a man
Lk 4:38-39	Fever in Simon Peter's mother-in-law
Lk 4:40-41	Various sicknesses and demons
Lk 5:4-7	Large catch of fish
Lk 5:12-14	Leper
Lk 5:15	Crowds healed of sicknesses
Lk 5:18-26	Paralytic brought from roof – forgiven sins and cured
Lk 6:6-10	Withered hand on the Sabbath
Lk 6:17-19	All diseases and impure spirits
Lk 7:1-10	Centurion's servant cured without Jesus going under master's roof
Lk 7:11-15	Widow's son brought to life
Lk 7:21	Diseases, evil spirits, and sight to blind
Lk 7:37-50	Sins from woman with perfume for Jesus

Lk 8:1-2	Evil spirits and diseases from Mary Magdalene and others
Lk 8:22-25	Calmed sea
Lk 8:26-39	Demons go out of Legion into pigs
Lk 8:41-42&8:49-56	Jairus' daughter brought to life
Lk 8:43-48	Hemorrhage in woman
Lk 9:11	All those who needed to be healed
Lk 9:12-17	Fed 5000 men with 5 loaves and 2 fish
Lk 9:28-36	Jesus is transfigured / God speaks – Son chosen – Listen to him.
Lk 9:37-43	Evil spirits from boy
Lk 11:14	Demon from a mute man
Lk 13:10-13	Woman crippled by spirit cured on Sabbath
Lk 14:1-4	Abnormal swelling healed on Sabbath
Lk 17:11-19	Ten lepers (one returned to give thanks)
Lk 18:35-43	Blind beggar
Lk 22:51	Severed ear
Jn 2:1-11	Changed water to wine at wedding
Jn 4:4-19	Jesus reveals a Samaritan woman's life
Jn 4:49-54	Official's son does not die
Jn 5:2-9	Invalid at Bethesda pool on Sabbath
Jn 6:2	Various sick
Jn 6:5-13	Fed 5000 men with 5 loaves and 2 fish
Jn 6:19-20	Jesus walks on water
Jn 9:1-41	Man born blind cured on Sabbath
Jn 11:1-44	Lazarus brought to life
Jn 12:28	God speaks – glorifying Jesus
Jn 21:1-14	Miraculous catch of fish

APPENDIX H

NAMES USED IN THIS BOOK

Advocate	Another term for Holy Spirit
Andrew	One of 12 apostles
Anna	A prophet
Apostles	The 12 closest followers to Jesus
Bartimaeus	Blind man who was cured
Beelzebul	Name given to prince of demons
Ceasar	Emperor of Rome
Centurian	Officer in Roman army over 100 soldiers
Chief priests	Those who supervised temple operations
Daniel	Prophet in early times
Devil	Satan – the evil one
Disciples	Followers of Jesus
Elijah	Early prophet
Elizabeth	Mother of John the Baptist
Father	Heavenly Father of Jesus - God
Gentiles	Non-Jews
God	Heavenly Father of Jesus - Almighty
Harodians	Followers of Harod, the tetrarch
Holy Spirit	Heavenly being with God and Jesus
Jairus	Leader of synagogue (Jewish church)

James	One of 12 apostles – brother of John
Jesus	Son of God – Savior of world
John the Baptist	Cousin of Jesus who baptized him
John	One of 12 apostles – brother of James
Joseph	Earthly father of Jesus
Judas	One of 12 apostles
Judas Iscariot	One of 12 apostles who betrayed Jesus
Lazarus	friend Jesus raised from the dead
Legion	Name of one unclean spirit
Levi	One of 12 apostles – also called Matthew
Lord	Another name for God or Jesus
Lot	Early Bible figure who turned to stone
Martha	A follower – sister of Mary
Mary	Mother of Jesus
Mary	Follower - sister of Martha
Mary Magdalene	Follower cured by Jesus
Matthew	One of 12 apostles – former tax collector
Messiah	Another term for Jesus, the Savior
Moses	Early figure given God's 10 commandments
Most High	God
Nicodemus	A Pharisee who came to Jesus at night
Peter	Top one of the 12 apostles
Pharisees	Laymen and clergy who applied laws
Philip	One of 12 apostles
Prophets	People who previously told future
Sadducees	Those with jurisdiction over religious matters
Samaritan	Resident of Samaria – a foreigner
Satan	The devil – the evil one

Shepherds	Those who tend sheep
Simon	Early name for Peter
Son of Man	A term for Jesus
Thomas	One of 12 apostles - doubted the resurrection
Twelve	The apostles – those closest to Jesus
Zebedee	Father of James and John
Zechariah	Father of John the Baptist

INDEX

NOTE:

Next to the verse number is a command number – not a page number. The first entry in the index is Mt 3:15 17. This refers to Matthew chapter 3 verse 15 in a Bible which is noted in this text in chapter 17. The command is "Do good deeds / be righteous."

If a letter is next to the verse number, the verse can be found in that letter of the appendix. For example, A5 refers to Appendix A part 5 – Thou shall not kill.

If a verse appears more than in one location in this book, the word "MULTI" is used to denote the multiple locations.

Mt 3:15	17	
Mt 3:15	33	MULTI
Mt 3:17	1	
Mt 3:17	24	MULTI
Mt 4:2	9	
Mt 4:4	21	
Mt 4:4	23	MULTI
Mt 4:7	24	
Mt 4:10	24	
Mt 4:10	A1	MULTI
Mt 4:17	32	
Mt 4:17	36	MULTI
Mt 4:18	15	
Mt 4:19	15	
Mt 4:21	15	
Mt 4:22	15	
Mt 4:23	36	
Mt 4:25	15	
Mt 5:3	D	
Mt 5:4	D	
Mt 5:5	18	
Mt 5:5	D	MULTI
Mt 5:6	17	
Mt 5:6	D	MULTI
Mt 5:7	16	
Mt 5:7	D	MULTI
Mt 5:8	7	
Mt 5:8	35	MULTI
Mt 5:8	D	MULTI
Mt 5:9	D	
Mt 5:10	17	
Mt 5:10	27	MULTI
Mt 5:10	D	MULTI
Mt 5:11	27	
Mt 5:11	D	MULTI
Mt 5:12	27	
Mt 5:12	D	MULTI
Mt 5:16	17	
Mt 5:19	21	
Mt 5:19	36	MULTI
Mt 5:20	13	
Mt 5:20	17	MULTI
Mt 5:21	A6	
Mt 5:22	8	
Mt 5:22	25	MULTI
Mt 5:22	35	MULTI
Mt 5:23	32	
Mt 5:24	32	
Mt 5:25	32	
Mt 5:27	A7	
Mt 5:28	A7	
Mt 5:29	11	
Mt 5:30	11	
Mt 5:32	10	
Mt 5:32	A7	MULTI
Mt 5:34	35	
Mt 5:35	35	
Mt 5:36	35	
Mt 5:37	35	
Mt 5:39	25	
Mt 5:40	25	
Mt 5:41	25	
Mt 5:42	25	
Mt 5:44	25	
Mt 5:44	27	MULTI
Mt 5:44	29	MULTI

Mt 5:48	8		Mt 6:34	40	
Mt 6:1	17		Mt 7:1	19	
Mt 6:2	25		Mt 7:2	19	
Mt 6:3	25		Mt 7:5	11	
Mt 6:4	25		Mt 7:5	31	MULTI
Mt 6:5	29		Mt 7:5	32	MULTI
Mt 6:6	29		Mt 7:6	38	
Mt 6:7	29		Mt 7:7	29	
Mt 6:8	29		Mt 7:11	29	
Mt 6:9	29		Mt 7:12	25	
Mt 6:9	B	MULTI	Mt 7:13	13	
Mt 6:10	B		Mt 7:14	13	
Mt 6:11	B		Mt 7:15	4	
Mt 6:12	16		Mt 7:19	3	
Mt 6:12	B	MULTI	Mt 7:19	11	MULTI
Mt 6:13	B		Mt 7:21	13	
Mt 6:14	16		Mt 7:21	39	MULTI
Mt 6:15	16		Mt 7:24	23	
Mt 6:16	9		Mt 7:26	23	
Mt 6:17	9		Mt 7:28	36	
Mt 6:18	9		Mt 7:29	36	
Mt 6:19	9		Mt 8:10	14	
Mt 6:20	9		Mt 8:13	14	
Mt 6:20	17	MULTI	Mt 8:22	15	
Mt 6:24	24		Mt 8:26	14	
Mt 6:24	A1	MULTI	Mt 9:2	14	
Mt 6:25	40		Mt 9:2	16	MULTI
Mt 6:28	22		Mt 9:6	14	
Mt 6:28	40	MULTI	Mt 9:6	16	MULTI
Mt 6:31	40		Mt 9:8	24	
Mt 6:33	17		Mt 9:9	15	
Mt 6:33	24	MULTI	Mt 9:13	16	
Mt 6:33	A1	MULTI	Mt 9:13	22	MULTI

Mt 9:15	9	
Mt 9:20	14	
Mt 9:21	14	
Mt 9:22	14	
Mt 9:29	14	
Mt 9:35	36	
Mt 9:38	29	
Mt 10:5	C	
Mt 10:6	C	
Mt 10:7	C	
Mt 10:8	C	
Mt 10:9	C	
Mt 10:10	C	
Mt 10:11	C	
Mt 10:12	C	
Mt 10:13	C	
Mt 10:14	23	
Mt 10:14	25	MULTI
Mt 10:14	C	MULTI
Mt 10:16	4	
Mt 10:16	C	MULTI
Mt 10:17	4	
Mt 10:17	C	MULTI
Mt 10:19	35	
Mt 10:19	40	MULTI
Mt 10:19	C	MULTI
Mt 10:22	12	
Mt 10:22	28	MULTI
Mt 10:22	C	MULTI
Mt 10:23	27	
Mt 10:23	C	MULTI
Mt 10:26	2	
Mt 10:26	C	MULTI
Mt 10:27	35	
Mt 10:27	C	MULTI
Mt 10:28	2	
Mt 10:28	C	MULTI
Mt 10:31	2	
Mt 10:31	C	MULTI
Mt 10:32	1	
Mt 10:33	1	
Mt 10:37	24	
Mt 10:38	8	
Mt 10:38	15	MULTI
Mt 10:39	27	
Mt 10:40	25	
Mt 10:41	17	
Mt 10:41	25	MULTI
Mt 10:42	25	
Mt 11:1	36	
Mt 11:6	24	
Mt 11:6	D	MULTI
Mt 11:14	23	
Mt 11:15	23	
Mt 11:20	32	
Mt 11:21	17	
Mt 11:21	32	MULTI
Mt 11:21	E	MULTI
Mt 11:23	17	
Mt 11:25	24	
Mt 11:25	35	MULTI
Mt 11:25	39	MULTI
Mt 11:26	39	
Mt 11:28	15	
Mt 11:29	15	
Mt 11:29	18	MULTI

Mt 11:29	22	MULTI
Mt 12:7	16	
Mt 12:12	A4	
Mt 12:13	A4	
Mt 12:31	5	
Mt 12:31	16	MULTI
Mt 12:32	5	
Mt 12:32	16	MULTI
Mt 12:33	3	
Mt 12:36	35	
Mt 12:37	35	
Mt 12:50	39	
Mt 13:8	3	
Mt 13:8	23	MULTI
Mt 13:9	23	
Mt 13:16	D	
Mt 13:18	23	
Mt 13:21	27	
Mt 13:21	28	MULTI
Mt 13:22	9	
Mt 13:22	40	MULTI
Mt 13:23	3	
Mt 13:23	23	MULTI
Mt 13:43	17	
Mt 13:43	23	MULTI
Mt 13:44	9	
Mt 13:45	9	
Mt 13:46	9	
Mt 13:54	36	
Mt 13:58	14	
Mt 14:19	37	
Mt 14:23	29	
Mt 14:27	2	
Mt 14:28	15	
Mt 14:29	15	
Mt 14:31	2	
Mt 14:31	14	MULTI
Mt 14:33	24	
Mt 15:4	A5	
Mt 15:10	23	
Mt 15:10	35	MULTI
Mt 15:11	23	
Mt 15:11	35	MULTI
Mt 15:18	35	
Mt 15:19	7	
Mt 15:19	8	MULTI
Mt 15:19	35	MULTI
Mt 15:19	A6	MULTI
Mt 15:19	A7	MULTI
Mt 15:19	A8	MULTI
Mt 15:19	A9	MULTI
Mt 15:20	7	
Mt 15:20	8	MULTI
Mt 15:20	35	MULTI
Mt 15:20	A6	MULTI
Mt 15:20	A7	MULTI
Mt 15:20	A8	MULTI
Mt 15:20	A9	MULTI
Mt 15:26	38	
Mt 15:28	14	
Mt 15:31	24	
Mt 15:36	37	
Mt 16:6	4	
Mt 16:8	14	
Mt 16:9	14	
Mt 16:11	4	

Mt 16:12	4	
Mt 16:19	16	
Mt 16:19	33	MULTI
Mt 16:19	C	MULTI
Mt 16:24	8	
Mt 16:24	9	MULTI
Mt 16:24	15	MULTI
Mt 16:25	27	
Mt 16:27	8	
Mt 17:5	1	
Mt 17:5	23	MULTI
Mt 17:7	2	
Mt 17:20	14	
Mt 18:3	13	
Mt 18:3	18	MULTI
Mt 18:4	18	
Mt 18:5	25	
Mt 18:6	6	
Mt 18:7	6	
Mt 18:7	E	MULTI
Mt 18:8	11	
Mt 18:9	11	
Mt 18:10	25	
Mt 18:15	31	
Mt 18:16	31	
Mt 18:17	31	
Mt 18:18	16	
Mt 18:18	33	MULTI
Mt 18:19	29	
Mt 18:21	16	
Mt 18:22	16	
Mt 18:34	16	
Mt 18:35	16	
Mt 19:6	10	
Mt 19:7	10	
Mt 19:8	10	
Mt 19:9	10	
Mt 19:9	A7	MULTI
Mt 19:13	29	
Mt 19:14	15	
Mt 19:14	18	MULTI
Mt 19:14	25	MULTI
Mt 19:16	25	
Mt 19:17	13	
Mt 19:17	21	MULTI
Mt 19:18	A6	
Mt 19:18	A7	MULTI
Mt 19:18	A8	MULTI
Mt 19:18	A9	MULTI
Mt 19:19	25	
Mt 19:19	26	MULTI
Mt 19:19	A5	MULTI
Mt 19:21	8	
Mt 19:21	9	MULTI
Mt 19:21	15	MULTI
Mt 19:21	25	MULTI
Mt 19:23	9	
Mt 19:24	9	
Mt 19:29	9	
Mt 20:26	34	
Mt 20:27	34	
Mt 20:28	25	
Mt 20:28	34	MULTI
Mt 21:12	31	
Mt 21:12	38	MULTI
Mt 21:21	14	

Mt 21:22	14	
Mt 21:22	29	MULTI
Mt 21:23	36	
Mt 21:32	14	
Mt 21:32	17	MULTI
Mt 21:32	32	MULTI
Mt 21:43	3	
Mt 22:16	36	
Mt 22:21	24	
Mt 22:21	25	MULTI
Mt 22:33	36	
Mt 22:37	24	
Mt 22:37	25	MULTI
Mt 22:37	26	MULTI
Mt 22:37	A1	MULTI
Mt 22:38	24	
Mt 22:38	25	MULTI
Mt 22:38	26	MULTI
Mt 22:38	A1	MULTI
Mt 22:39	24	
Mt 22:39	25	MULTI
Mt 22:39	26	MULTI
Mt 22:39	A1	MULTI
Mt 22:40	24	
Mt 22:40	25	MULTI
Mt 22:40	26	MULTI
Mt 22:40	A1	MULTI
Mt 23:3	8	
Mt 23:8	24	
Mt 23:9	24	
Mt 23:9	A1	MULTI
Mt 23:10	24	
Mt 23:11	34	
Mt 23:12	18	
Mt 23:13	E	
Mt 23:15	E	
Mt 23:16	E	
Mt 23:20	35	
Mt 23:21	35	
Mt 23:22	35	
Mt 23:23	14	
Mt 23:23	16	MULTI
Mt 23:23	20	MULTI
Mt 23:23	21	MULTI
Mt 23:23	A1	MULTI
Mt 23:23	E	MULTI
Mt 23:25	9	
Mt 23:25	E	MULTI
Mt 23:27	E	
Mt 23:28	17	
Mt 23:29	E	
Mt 24:4	4	
Mt 24:4	12	MULTI
Mt 24:6	2	
Mt 24:6	12	MULTI
Mt 24:9	27	
Mt 24:13	12	
Mt 24:13	28	MULTI
Mt 24:15	12	
Mt 24:16	12	
Mt 24:17	12	
Mt 24:18	12	
Mt 24:19	E	
Mt 24:20	12	
Mt 24:20	29	MULTI
Mt 24:23	12	

Mt 24:23	14	MULTI		Mt 26:26	33	
Mt 24:26	12			Mt 26:26	37	MULTI
Mt 24:26	14	MULTI		Mt 26:27	33	
Mt 24:27	14			Mt 26:27	37	MULTI
Mt 24:32	12			Mt 26:28	33	
Mt 24:32	22	MULTI		Mt 26:28	37	MULTI
Mt 24:33	12			Mt 26:36	29	
Mt 24:33	22	MULTI		Mt 26:38	30	
Mt 24:42	12			Mt 26:39	29	
Mt 24:42	30	MULTI		Mt 26:39	39	MULTI
Mt 24:43	12			Mt 26:41	12	
Mt 24:43	30	MULTI		Mt 26:41	29	MULTI
Mt 24:44	12			Mt 26:41	30	MULTI
Mt 24:44	30	MULTI		Mt 26:42	29	
Mt 24:46	12			Mt 26:42	39	MULTI
Mt 24:46	30	MULTI		Mt 26:44	29	
Mt 24:46	34	MULTI		Mt 26:44	39	MULTI
Mt 24:46	D	MULTI		Mt 26:55	36	
Mt 24:50	12			Mt 28:10	2	
Mt 24:50	30	MULTI		Mt 28:10	15	MULTI
Mt 25:13	12			Mt 28:19	33	
Mt 25:13	30	MULTI		Mt 28:19	36	MULTI
Mt 25:40	8			Mt 28:19	C	MULTI
Mt 25:40	17	MULTI		Mt 28:20	21	
Mt 25:40	25	MULTI		Mt 28:20	36	MULTI
Mt 25:45	8			Mt 28:20	C	MULTI
Mt 25:45	17	MULTI				
Mt 25:45	25	MULTI		Mk 1:9	33	
Mt 25:46	8			Mk 1:11	1	
Mt 25:46	17	MULTI		Mk 1:11	24	MULTI
Mt 25:46	25	MULTI		Mk 1:14	36	
Mt 26:13	24			Mk 1:15	14	
Mt 26:24	E			Mk 1:15	32	MULTI

Mk 1:16	15	
Mk 1:17	15	
Mk 1:19	15	
Mk 1:20	15	
Mk 1:21	36	
Mk 1:21	A4	MULTI
Mk 1:24	1	
Mk 1:35	29	
Mk 1:38	36	
Mk 1:39	36	
Mk 2:2	36	
Mk 2:4	14	
Mk 2:5	14	
Mk 2:5	16	MULTI
Mk 2:10	16	
Mk 2:11	16	
Mk 2:12	24	
Mk 2:13	36	
Mk 2:14	15	
Mk 2:20	9	
Mk 2:27	A4	
Mk 2:28	A4	
Mk 3:4	A4	
Mk 3:5	A4	
Mk 3:11	1	
Mk 3:14	36	
Mk 3:28	5	
Mk 3:28	16	MULTI
Mk 3:29	5	
Mk 3:29	16	MULTI
Mk 3:35	39	
Mk 4:1	36	
Mk 4:3	23	
Mk 4:8	3	
Mk 4:8	23	MULTI
Mk 4:9	3	
Mk 4:9	23	MULTI
Mk 4:17	27	
Mk 4:17	28	MULTI
Mk 4:18	9	
Mk 4:18	40	MULTI
Mk 4:19	9	
Mk 4:19	40	MULTI
Mk 4:20	3	
Mk 4:20	23	MULTI
Mk 4:22	23	
Mk 4:23	23	
Mk 4:24	23	
Mk 4:24	25	MULTI
Mk 4:33	36	
Mk 4:40	2	
Mk 4:40	14	MULTI
Mk 5:7	1	
Mk 5:19	16	
Mk 5:34	14	
Mk 5:36	2	
Mk 5:36	14	MULTI
Mk 6:2	36	
Mk 6:2	A4	MULTI
Mk 6:6	14	
Mk 6:6	36	MULTI
Mk 6:7	C	
Mk 6:8	C	
Mk 6:9	C	
Mk 6:10	C	
Mk 6:11	25	

Mk 6:11	C	MULTI		Mk 7:22	A8	MULTI
Mk 6:31	15			Mk 7:22	A9	MULTI
Mk 6:34	36			Mk 7:22	A10	MULTI
Mk 6:41	37			Mk 7:23	7	
Mk 6:46	29			Mk 7:23	8	MULTI
Mk 6:50	2			Mk 7:23	9	MULTI
Mk 7:8	21			Mk 7:23	18	MULTI
Mk 7:10	A5			Mk 7:23	25	MULTI
Mk 7:14	8			Mk 7:23	35	MULTI
Mk 7:14	23	MULTI		Mk 7:23	A6	MULTI
Mk 7:14	35	MULTI		Mk 7:23	A7	MULTI
Mk 7:15	8			Mk 7:23	A8	MULTI
Mk 7:15	23	MULTI		Mk 7:23	A9	MULTI
Mk 7:15	35	MULTI		Mk 7:23	A10	MULTI
Mk 7:21	7			Mk 7:27	38	
Mk 7:21	8	MULTI		Mk 8:6	37	
Mk 7:21	9	MULTI		Mk 8:7	37	
Mk 7:21	18	MULTI		Mk 8:15	4	
Mk 7:21	25	MULTI		Mk 8:31	36	
Mk 7:21	35	MULTI		Mk 8:34	8	
Mk 7:21	A6	MULTI		Mk 8:34	9	MULTI
Mk 7:21	A7	MULTI		Mk 8:34	15	MULTI
Mk 7:21	A8	MULTI		Mk 8:35	27	
Mk 7:21	A9	MULTI		Mk 8:38	1	
Mk 7:21	A10	MUL		Mk 9:7	1	
Mk 7:22	7			Mk 9:7	23	MULTI
Mk 7:22	8	MULTI		Mk 9:7	24	MULTI
Mk 7:22	9	MULTI		Mk 9:23	14	
Mk 7:22	18	MULTI		Mk 9:24	14	
Mk 7:22	25	MULTI		Mk 9:29	29	
Mk 7:22	35	MULTI		Mk 9:31	36	
Mk 7:22	A6	MULTI		Mk 9:35	34	
Mk 7:22	A7	MULTI		Mk 9:37	25	

Mk 9:41	25	
Mk 9:42	6	
Mk 9:43	11	
Mk 9:45	11	
Mk 9:47	11	
Mk 9:50	8	
Mk 9:50	28	MULTI
Mk 10:1	36	
Mk 10:9	10	
Mk 10:11	10	
Mk 10:11	A7	MULTI
Mk 10:12	10	
Mk 10:12	A7	MULTI
Mk 10:13	15	
Mk 10:13	18	MULTI
Mk 10:13	25	MULTI
Mk 10:14	15	
Mk 10:14	18	MULTI
Mk 10:14	25	MULTI
Mk 10:15	13	
Mk 10:15	14	MULTI
Mk 10:15	18	MULTI
Mk 10:15	25	MULTI
Mk 10:19	8	
Mk 10:19	21	MULTI
Mk 10:19	A5	MULTI
Mk 10:19	A6	MULTI
Mk 10:19	A7	MULTI
Mk 10:19	A8	MULTI
Mk 10:19	A9	MULTI
Mk 10:21	9	
Mk 10:21	15	MULTI
Mk 10:21	25	MULTI
Mk 10:23	9	
Mk 10:25	9	
Mk 10:29	9	
Mk 10:29	27	MULTI
Mk 10:30	9	
Mk 10:30	27	MULTI
Mk 10:43	34	
Mk 10:44	34	
Mk 10:45	34	
Mk 10:52	14	
Mk 10:52	15	MULTI
Mk 11:15	38	
Mk 11:16	38	
Mk 11:17	36	
Mk 11:18	36	
Mk 11:22	14	
Mk 11:23	14	
Mk 11:24	14	
Mk 11:24	29	MULTI
Mk 11:25	16	
Mk 11:25	29	MULTI
Mk 12:9	8	
Mk 12:14	36	
Mk 12:17	24	
Mk 12:17	25	MULTI
Mk 12:29	23	
Mk 12:29	24	MULTI
Mk 12:29	25	MULTI
Mk 12:29	26	MULTI
Mk 12:29	A1	MULTI
Mk 12:30	23	
Mk 12:30	24	MULTI
Mk 12:30	25	MULTI

Mk 12:30	26	MULTI	Mk 13:5	4	
Mk 12:30	A1	MULTI	Mk 13:5	12	MULTI
Mk 12:31	23		Mk 13:7	2	
Mk 12:31	24	MULTI	Mk 13:7	12	MULTI
Mk 12:31	25	MULTI	Mk 13:9	4	
Mk 12:31	26	MULTI	Mk 13:9	12	MULTI
Mk 12:31	A1	MULTI	Mk 13:11	12	
Mk 12:32	23		Mk 13:11	35	MULTI
Mk 12:32	24	MULTI	Mk 13:11	40	MULTI
Mk 12:32	25	MULTI	Mk 13:13	12	
Mk 12:32	26	MULTI	Mk 13:13	28	MULTI
Mk 12:32	A1	MULTI	Mk 13:14	12	
Mk 12:33	23		Mk 13:15	12	
Mk 12:33	24	MULTI	Mk 13:16	12	
Mk 12:33	25	MULTI	Mk 13:17	E	
Mk 12:33	26	MULTI	Mk 13:18	12	
Mk 12:33	A1	MULTI	Mk 13:18	29	MULTI
Mk 12:34	23		Mk 13:21	12	
Mk 12:34	24	MULTI	Mk 13:21	14	MULTI
Mk 12:34	25	MULTI	Mk 13:23	4	
Mk 12:34	26	MULTI	Mk 13:23	12	MULTI
Mk 12:34	A1	MULTI	Mk 13:28	12	
Mk 12:35	36		Mk 13:28	22	MULTI
Mk 12:38	4		Mk 13:29	12	
Mk 12:38	36	MULTI	Mk 13:29	22	MULTI
Mk 12:39	4		Mk 13:33	4	
Mk 12:39	36	MULTI	Mk 13:33	12	MULTI
Mk 12:40	4		Mk 13:33	30	MULTI
Mk 12:40	29	MULTI	Mk 13:35	12	
Mk 12:40	36	MULTI	Mk 13:35	30	MULTI
Mk 12:44	9		Mk 13:36	12	
Mk 12:44	24	MULTI	Mk 13:36	30	MULTI
Mk 13:4	12		Mk 13:37	12	

Mk 13:37	30	MULTI		Lk 1:58	16	
Mk 14:9	24			Lk 1:64	24	
Mk 14:21	E			Lk 1:68	24	
Mk 14:22	33			Lk 1:72	16	
Mk 14:22	37	MULTI		Lk 1:74	17	
Mk 14:23	33			Lk 1:75	17	
Mk 14:23	37	MULTI		Lk 1:78	16	
Mk 14:27	14			Lk 2:10	2	
Mk 14:29	14			Lk 2:14	24	
Mk 14:32	29			Lk 2:20	24	
Mk 14:34	30			Lk 2:37	9	
Mk 14:35	29			Lk 2:37	24	MULTI
Mk 14:36	39			Lk 2:37	29	MULTI
Mk 14:38	29			Lk 2:38	37	
Mk 14:38	30	MULTI		Lk 3:3	36	
Mk 14:39	29			Lk 3:21	1	
Mk 14:49	36			Lk 3:21	24	MULTI
Mk 16:14	14			Lk 3:21	29	MULTI
Mk 16:14	31	MULTI		Lk 3:21	33	MULTI
Mk 16:15	36			Lk 3:22	1	
Mk 16:16	14			Lk 3:22	24	MULTI
Mk 16:16	33	MULTI		Lk 3:22	29	MULTI
				Lk 3:22	33	MULTI
Lk 1:46	24			Lk 4:4	21	
Lk 1:47	24			Lk 4:4	23	MULTI
Lk 1:48	18			Lk 4:8	24	
Lk 1:48	D	MULTI		Lk 4:8	A1	MULTI
Lk 1:49	24			Lk 4:12	24	
Lk 1:50	16			Lk 4:15	36	
Lk 1:51	35			Lk 4:16	36	
Lk 1:52	18			Lk 4:17	36	
Lk 1:54	16			Lk 4:18	36	
Lk 1:57	16			Lk 4:19	36	

Lk 4:20	36			Lk 6:24	E	
Lk 4:21	36			Lk 6:25	E	
Lk 4:31	36			Lk 6:26	E	
Lk 4:31	A4	MULTI		Lk 6:27	17	
Lk 4:32	36			Lk 6:27	23	MULTI
Lk 4:43	36			Lk 6:27	25	MULTI
Lk 4:44	36			Lk 6:27	29	MULTI
Lk 5:3	36			Lk 6:28	17	
Lk 5:10	2			Lk 6:28	23	MULTI
Lk 5:11	15			Lk 6:28	25	MULTI
Lk 5:15	23			Lk 6:28	29	MULTI
Lk 5:15	36	MULTI		Lk 6:29	17	
Lk 5:16	29			Lk 6:29	25	MULTI
Lk 5:17	36			Lk 6:30	17	
Lk 5:20	14			Lk 6:30	25	MULTI
Lk 5:20	16	MULTI		Lk 6:31	17	
Lk 5:24	16			Lk 6:31	25	MULTI
Lk 5:25	24			Lk 6:35	17	
Lk 5:25	37	MULTI		Lk 6:35	25	MULTI
Lk 5:26	24			Lk 6:36	16	
Lk 5:27	15			Lk 6:37	16	
Lk 5:32	32			Lk 6:37	19	MULTI
Lk 5:35	9			Lk 6:38	25	
Lk 6:5	A4			Lk 6:42	31	
Lk 6:6	36			Lk 6:42	32	MULTI
Lk 6:6	A4	MULTI		Lk 6:45	17	
Lk 6:9	A4			Lk 6:45	35	MULTI
Lk 6:10	A4			Lk 6:46	21	
Lk 6:12	29			Lk 6:47	23	
Lk 6:20	D			Lk 6:48	23	
Lk 6:21	D			Lk 6:49	23	
Lk 6:22	D			Lk 7:1	36	
Lk 6:23	D			Lk 7:9	14	

Lk 7:10	14	
Lk 7:16	24	
Lk 7:23	5	
Lk 7:23	24	MULTI
Lk 7:23	D	MULTI
Lk 7:24	36	
Lk 7:44	24	
Lk 7:45	24	
Lk 7:46	24	
Lk 7:47	16	
Lk 7:47	24	MULTI
Lk 7:48	16	
Lk 7:50	14	
Lk 8:1	36	
Lk 8:8	3	
Lk 8:8	23	MULTI
Lk 8:15	3	
Lk 8:15	23	MULTI
Lk 8:15	28	MULTI
Lk 8:18	23	
Lk 8:21	23	
Lk 8:25	14	
Lk 8:38	24	
Lk 8:39	24	
Lk 8:48	14	
Lk 8:49	2	
Lk 8:49	14	MULTI
Lk 8:50	2	
Lk 8:50	14	MULTI
Lk 9:1	C	
Lk 9:2	36	
Lk 9:2	C	MULTI
Lk 9:3	C	
Lk 9:4	C	
Lk 9:5	C	
Lk 9:6	36	
Lk 9:11	15	
Lk 9:11	25	MULTI
Lk 9:11	36	MULTI
Lk 9:16	37	
Lk 9:18	29	
Lk 9:23	8	
Lk 9:23	9	MULTI
Lk 9:23	15	MULTI
Lk 9:24	27	
Lk 9:26	1	
Lk 9:28	29	
Lk 9:29	29	
Lk 9:35	1	
Lk 9:35	23	MULTI
Lk 9:44	23	
Lk 9:48	18	
Lk 9:55	31	
Lk 9:59	9	
Lk 9:59	15	MULTI
Lk 9:59	36	MULTI
Lk 9:60	9	
Lk 9:60	15	MULTI
Lk 9:60	36	MULTI
Lk 9:61	9	
Lk 9:61	15	MULTI
Lk 9:62	9	
Lk 9:62	15	MULTI
Lk 10:1	C	
Lk 10:2	29	
Lk 10:2	C	MULTI

Lk 10:3	36			Lk 10:37	25	MULTI
Lk 10:3	C	MULTI		Lk 10:39	23	
Lk 10:4	C			Lk 10:39	40	MULTI
Lk 10:5	C			Lk 10:40	23	
Lk 10:7	C			Lk 10:40	40	MULTI
Lk 10:8	36			Lk 10:41	23	
Lk 10:8	C	MULTI		Lk 10:41	40	MULTI
Lk 10:9	36			Lk 10:42	23	
Lk 10:9	C	MULTI		Lk 10:42	40	MULTI
Lk 10:10	36			Lk 11:1	29	
Lk 10:10	C	MULTI		Lk 11:2	29	
Lk 10:11	36			Lk 11:2	B	MULTI
Lk 10:11	C	MULTI		Lk 11:3	B	
Lk 10:12	C			Lk 11:4	16	
Lk 10:13	E			Lk 11:4	B	MULTI
Lk 10:16	1			Lk 11:8	28	
Lk 10:16	23	MULTI		Lk 11:9	29	
Lk 10:20	37			Lk 11:10	29	
Lk 10:21	24			Lk 11:13	25	
Lk 10:23	D			Lk 11:13	29	MULTI
Lk 10:27	24			Lk 11:17	8	
Lk 10:27	25	MULTI		Lk 11:27	23	
Lk 10:27	26	MULTI		Lk 11:27	D	MULTI
Lk 10:27	A1	MULTI		Lk 11:28	21	
Lk 10:28	24			Lk 11:28	23	MULTI
Lk 10:28	25	MULTI		Lk 11:28	D	MULTI
Lk 10:28	26	MULTI		Lk 11:35	8	
Lk 10:28	A1	MULTI		Lk 11:35	26	MULTI
Lk 10:36	16			Lk 11:41	25	
Lk 10:36	17	MULTI		Lk 11:42	20	
Lk 10:36	25	MULTI		Lk 11:42	24	MULTI
Lk 10:37	16			Lk 11:42	A1	MULTI
Lk 10:37	17	MULTI		Lk 11:42	E	MULTI

Lk 11:43	E		Lk 12:36	30	MULTI
Lk 11:44	E		Lk 12:37	12	
Lk 11:46	E		Lk 12:37	30	MULTI
Lk 11:47	E		Lk 12:37	D	MULTI
Lk 11:52	E		Lk 12:38	12	
Lk 12:1	4		Lk 12:38	30	MULTI
Lk 12:4	2		Lk 12:38	D	MULTI
Lk 12:5	2		Lk 12:40	12	
Lk 12:7	2		Lk 12:40	30	MULTI
Lk 12:8	1		Lk 12:43	12	
Lk 12:9	1		Lk 12:43	30	MULTI
Lk 12:10	5		Lk 12:43	D	MULTI
Lk 12:10	16	MULTI	Lk 12:46	12	
Lk 12:11	35		Lk 12:46	30	MULTI
Lk 12:11	40	MULTI	Lk 12:47	12	
Lk 12:12	35		Lk 12:47	30	MULTI
Lk 12:12	40	MULTI	Lk 12:47	39	MULTI
Lk 12:15	4		Lk 12:48	12	
Lk 12:15	9	MULTI	Lk 12:48	30	MULTI
Lk 12:21	9		Lk 12:48	39	MULTI
Lk 12:21	24	MULTI	Lk 12:58	32	
Lk 12:21	A1	MULTI	Lk 13:3	32	
Lk 12:22	40		Lk 13:5	32	
Lk 12:25	40		Lk 13:8	3	
Lk 12:26	40		Lk 13:8	11	MULTI
Lk 12:28	14		Lk 13:9	3	
Lk 12:29	40		Lk 13:9	11	MULTI
Lk 12:31	24		Lk 13:10	36	
Lk 12:31	A1	MULTI	Lk 13:10	A4	MULTI
Lk 12:32	2		Lk 13:13	24	
Lk 12:33	9		Lk 13:13	37	MULTI
Lk 12:33	25	MULTI	Lk 13:13	A4	MULTI
Lk 12:36	12		Lk 13:22	36	

Lk 13:24	13			Lk 17:3	31	MULTI
Lk 14:3	A4			Lk 17:3	32	MULTI
Lk 14:4	A4			Lk 17:4	16	
Lk 14:11	18			Lk 17:4	32	MULTI
Lk 14:13	25			Lk 17:6	14	
Lk 14:13	D	MULTI		Lk 17:10	21	
Lk 14:14	25			Lk 17:15	24	
Lk 14:14	D	MULTI		Lk 17:16	37	
Lk 14:26	9			Lk 17:18	24	
Lk 14:26	15	MULTI		Lk 17:18	37	MULTI
Lk 14:27	8			Lk 17:19	14	
Lk 14:27	15	MULTI		Lk 17:23	12	
Lk 14:33	9			Lk 17:31	12	
Lk 14:34	23			Lk 17:32	12	
Lk 14:34	28	MULTI		Lk 17:33	12	
Lk 14:35	23			Lk 17:33	27	MULTI
Lk 14:35	28	MULTI		Lk 18:1	28	
Lk 15:1	23			Lk 18:1	29	MULTI
Lk 15:7	32			Lk 18:5	23	
Lk 15:10	32			Lk 18:5	28	MULTI
Lk 16:9	38			Lk 18:5	29	MULTI
Lk 16:10	38			Lk 18:6	23	
Lk 16:11	38			Lk 18:6	28	MULTI
Lk 16:12	38			Lk 18:6	29	MULTI
Lk 16:13	24			Lk 18:7	28	
Lk 16:13	A1	MULTI		Lk 18:7	29	MULTI
Lk 16:18	10			Lk 18:8	28	
Lk 16:18	A7	MULTI		Lk 18:8	29	MULTI
Lk 17:1	6			Lk 18:10	16	
Lk 17:1	E	MULTI		Lk 18:10	18	MULTI
Lk 17:2	6			Lk 18:10	29	MULTI
Lk 17:3	16			Lk 18:14	16	
Lk 17:3	30	MULTI		Lk 18:14	18	MULTI

Lk 18:14	29	MULTI		Lk 19:45	38	
Lk 18:16	15			Lk 19:47	36	
Lk 18:16	18	MULTI		Lk 20:1	36	
Lk 18:16	25	MULTI		Lk 20:21	36	
Lk 18:17	13			Lk 20:25	24	
Lk 18:17	14	MULTI		Lk 20:25	25	MULTI
Lk 18:17	18	MULTI		Lk 20:46	4	
Lk 18:20	21			Lk 21:4	24	
Lk 18:20	A5	MULTI		Lk 21:8	4	
Lk 18:20	A6	MULTI		Lk 21:8	12	MULTI
Lk 18:20	A7	MULTI		Lk 21:9	2	
Lk 18:20	A8	MULTI		Lk 21:9	12	MULTI
Lk 18:20	A9	MULTI		Lk 21:14	12	
Lk 18:22	9			Lk 21:14	35	MULTI
Lk 18:22	15	MULTI		Lk 21:14	40	MULTI
Lk 18:22	25	MULTI		Lk 21:15	12	
Lk 18:24	9			Lk 21:15	35	MULTI
Lk 18:25	9			Lk 21:15	40	MULTI
Lk 18:29	9			Lk 21:19	28	
Lk 18:30	9			Lk 21:20	12	
Lk 18:42	14			Lk 21:21	12	
Lk 18:43	15			Lk 21:23	E	
Lk 18:43	24	MULTI		Lk 21:28	12	
Lk 18:43	37	MULTI		Lk 21:31	12	
Lk 19:10	16			Lk 21:31	22	MULTI
Lk 19:17	34			Lk 21:32	22	
Lk 19:17	38	MULTI		Lk 21:34	4	
Lk 19:19	34			Lk 21:34	9	MULTI
Lk 19:19	38	MULTI		Lk 21:34	12	MULTI
Lk 19:37	17			Lk 21:34	40	MULTI
Lk 19:37	24	MULTI		Lk 21:35	4	
Lk 19:37	37	MULTI		Lk 21:35	9	MULTI
Lk 19:38	D			Lk 21:35	12	MULTI

Lk 21:35	40	MULTI		Lk 24:36	40	MULTI
Lk 21:36	4			Lk 24:38	2	
Lk 21:36	12	MULTI		Lk 24:38	40	MULTI
Lk 21:36	29	MULTI		Lk 24:47	32	
Lk 21:36	30	MULTI		Lk 24:47	36	MULTI
Lk 21:37	36			Lk 24:50	37	
Lk 21:38	23			Lk 24:52	24	
Lk 22:17	33			Lk 24:53	24	
Lk 22:17	37	MULTI				
Lk 22:19	33			Jn 1:12	14	
Lk 22:19	37	MULTI		Jn 1:29	1	
Lk 22:20	33			Jn 1:37	15	
Lk 22:22	E			Jn 1:39	15	
Lk 22:26	34			Jn 1:43	15	
Lk 22:27	34			Jn 1:50	14	
Lk 22:32	14			Jn 2:11	14	
Lk 22:32	29	MULTI		Jn 2:15	31	
Lk 22:32	36	MULTI		Jn 2:15	38	MULTI
Lk 22:36	C			Jn 2:16	31	
Lk 22:40	29			Jn 2:16	38	MULTI
Lk 22:41	29			Jn 2:22	14	
Lk 22:42	29			Jn 2:23	14	
Lk 22:42	39	MULTI		Jn 3:2	36	
Lk 22:44	29			Jn 3:5	13	
Lk 22:46	29			Jn 3:5	33	MULTI
Lk 23:5	36			Jn 3:15	14	
Lk 23:28	25			Jn 3:16	14	
Lk 23:29	D			Jn 3:18	14	
Lk 23:34	16			Jn 3:21	17	
Lk 23:46	24			Jn 3:22	33	
Lk 23:46	29	MULTI		Jn 3:26	33	
Lk 24:30	37			Jn 3:36	14	
Lk 24:36	2			Jn 4:1	33	

Jn 4:2	33		Jn 6:43	8	
Jn 4:21	14		Jn 6:43	35	MULTI
Jn 4:23	24		Jn 6:45	22	
Jn 4:24	24		Jn 6:45	23	MULTI
Jn 4:34	39		Jn 6:45	36	MULTI
Jn 4:39	14		Jn 6:47	14	
Jn 4:41	14		Jn 6:51	33	
Jn 4:42	14		Jn 6:53	33	
Jn 4:53	14		Jn 6:54	33	
Jn 5:9	A4		Jn 6:56	33	
Jn 5:14	8		Jn 6:57	33	
Jn 5:22	19		Jn 6:58	33	
Jn 5:22	24	MULTI	Jn 6:59	36	
Jn 5:23	24		Jn 6:65	15	
Jn 5:24	14		Jn 6:68	14	
Jn 5:24	23	MULTI	Jn 6:69	14	
Jn 5:27	19		Jn 7:14	36	
Jn 5:28	17		Jn 7:16	36	
Jn 5:29	17		Jn 7:17	39	
Jn 5:30	20		Jn 7:24	19	
Jn 5:30	39	MULTI	Jn 7:28	36	
Jn 5:46	14		Jn 7:29	36	
Jn 6:11	37		Jn 7:31	14	
Jn 6:20	2		Jn 7:37	15	
Jn 6:23	37		Jn 7:38	14	
Jn 6:27	33		Jn 8:2	36	
Jn 6:29	14		Jn 8:7	19	
Jn 6:35	14		Jn 8:7	A7	MULTI
Jn 6:35	15	MULTI	Jn 8:10	19	
Jn 6:38	39		Jn 8:10	A7	MULTI
Jn 6:39	39		Jn 8:11	19	
Jn 6:40	14		Jn 8:11	A7	MULTI
Jn 6:40	39	MULTI	Jn 8:12	15	

Jn 8:12	36	MULTI	Jn 10:27	15	
Jn 8:15	19		Jn 10:27	23	MULTI
Jn 8:15	20	MULTI	Jn 10:37	14	
Jn 8:16	19		Jn 10:38	14	
Jn 8:20	36		Jn 10:42	14	
Jn 8:24	14		Jn 11:15	14	
Jn 8:28	39		Jn 11:25	14	
Jn 8:29	39		Jn 11:26	14	
Jn 8:30	14		Jn 11:27	14	
Jn 8:31	14		Jn 11:40	14	
Jn 8:31	21	MULTI	Jn 11:41	37	
Jn 8:31	23	MULTI	Jn 11:42	14	
Jn 8:32	14		Jn 11:42	23	MULTI
Jn 8:32	21	MULTI	Jn 11:45	14	
Jn 8:32	23	MULTI	Jn 12:11	14	
Jn 8:34	8		Jn 12:24	3	
Jn 8:46	14		Jn 12:25	27	
Jn 8:51	21		Jn 12:26	15	
Jn 8:51	23	MULTI	Jn 12:26	34	MULTI
Jn 8:55	21		Jn 12:28	1	
Jn 8:55	23	MULTI	Jn 12:28	23	MULTI
Jn 9:14	A4		Jn 12:30	23	
Jn 9:31	39		Jn 12:35	13	
Jn 9:38	14		Jn 12:35	14	MULTI
Jn 9:38	24	MULTI	Jn 12:36	14	
Jn 10:1	13		Jn 12:42	14	
Jn 10:2	13		Jn 12:44	14	
Jn 10:7	13		Jn 12:46	14	
Jn 10:9	13		Jn 12:47	19	
Jn 10:11	27		Jn 12:47	23	MULTI
Jn 10:15	27		Jn 12:48	19	
Jn 10:17	27		Jn 12:48	21	MULTI
Jn 10:18	27		Jn 12:48	23	MULTI

Jn 12:50	21	
Jn 13:13	36	
Jn 13:15	8	
Jn 13:15	15	MULTI
Jn 13:15	25	MULTI
Jn 13:16	34	
Jn 13:16	D	MULTI
Jn 13:17	34	
Jn 13:17	D	MULTI
Jn 13:20	14	
Jn 13:20	25	MULTI
Jn 13:34	25	
Jn 13:36	15	
Jn 14:1	14	
Jn 14:1	40	MULTI
Jn 14:6	13	
Jn 14:11	14	
Jn 14:12	14	
Jn 14:13	29	
Jn 14:14	29	
Jn 14:15	21	
Jn 14:15	24	MULTI
Jn 14:16	33	
Jn 14:17	33	
Jn 14:21	21	
Jn 14:21	24	MULTI
Jn 14:23	21	
Jn 14:23	24	MULTI
Jn 14:27	2	
Jn 14:27	25	MULTI
Jn 14:27	40	MULTI
Jn 14:28	14	
Jn 14:28	24	MULTI
Jn 14:29	14	
Jn 14:31	21	
Jn 14:31	24	MULTI
Jn 14:31	39	MULTI
Jn 15:4	3	
Jn 15:4	28	MULTI
Jn 15:5	3	
Jn 15:5	28	MULTI
Jn 15:7	28	
Jn 15:7	29	MULTI
Jn 15:8	3	
Jn 15:8	15	MULTI
Jn 15:8	24	MULTI
Jn 15:9	24	
Jn 15:9	28	MULTI
Jn 15:10	21	
Jn 15:10	24	MULTI
Jn 15:10	28	MULTI
Jn 15:12	25	
Jn 15:13	25	
Jn 15:13	27	MULTI
Jn 15:14	21	
Jn 15:16	3	
Jn 15:16	24	MULTI
Jn 15:16	29	MULTI
Jn 15:17	25	
Jn 15:20	27	
Jn 15:27	36	
Jn 16:8	14	
Jn 16:8	17	MULTI
Jn 16:8	20	MULTI
Jn 16:9	14	
Jn 16:10	17	

Jn 16:11	20	
Jn 16:23	29	
Jn 16:24	29	
Jn 16:27	14	
Jn 16:27	24	MULTI
Jn 16:30	14	
Jn 16:33	2	
Jn 16:33	40	MULTI
Jn 17:1	24	
Jn 17:1	29	MULTI
Jn 17:3	14	
Jn 17:6	21	
Jn 17:6	23	MULTI
Jn 17:8	1	
Jn 17:8	14	MULTI
Jn 17:8	23	MULTI
Jn 17:9	29	
Jn 17:15	29	
Jn 17:20	14	
Jn 17:20	29	MULTI
Jn 17:21	14	
Jn 18:20	36	
Jn 19:35	14	
Jn 20:19	2	
Jn 20:21	2	
Jn 20:21	33	MULTI
Jn 20:21	36	MULTI
Jn 20:22	33	
Jn 20:23	16	
Jn 20:23	33	MULTI
Jn 20:26	2	
Jn 20:27	14	
Jn 20:29	14	

Jn 20:29	D	MULTI
Jn 20:31	14	
Jn 21:15	24	
Jn 21:15	C	MULTI
Jn 21:16	24	
Jn 21:16	C	MULTI
Jn 21:17	24	
Jn 21:17	C	MULTI
Jn 21:18	15	
Jn 21:19	15	
Jn 21:22	15	

COMMANDS BY CATEGORY

NO. **GOD**

1. DO <u>ACKNOWLEDGE</u> JESUS
5. DON'T <u>BLASPHEME</u>
14. DO HAVE <u>FAITH</u>/BELIEVE
15. DO <u>FOLLOW</u>/COME
21. DO <u>KEEP THE COMMANDMENTS</u>
23. <u>LISTEN</u>/ACT ON GOD'S WORD
24. DO <u>LOVE GOD/JESUS</u>
29. DO <u>PRAY</u>/ASK
37. DO GIVE <u>THANKS</u>/ASK BLESSING
39. DO GOD'S <u>WILL</u>

OTHERS

6. DON'T <u>CAUSE</u> OTHERS TO SIN
10. DON'T <u>DIVORCE</u>
16. DO <u>FORGIVE</u>/HAVE MERCY
19. DON'T <u>JUDGE</u>/CONDEMN
25. DO <u>LOVE YOUR NEIGHBOR</u>
31. DO <u>REBUKE</u> WRONGDOERS
36. DO <u>TEACH</u>/PREACH

NO.	**SELF**
2.	DON'T BE <u>AFRAID</u>
3.	DO <u>BEAR</u> GOOD FRUIT
4.	DO <u>BEWARE</u>
7.	DO BE <u>CHASTE</u>
8.	DO HAVE GOOD <u>CONDUCT</u>
9.	DO <u>DENY</u> SELF / LEAVE TIES
11.	DO <u>ELIMINATE</u> IF BAD
13.	DO <u>ENTER</u> BY NARROW GATE
17.	DO <u>GOOD DEEDS</u>/RIGHTEOUS
18.	DO BE <u>HUMBLE</u>/MEEK
20.	DO HAVE RIGHT <u>JUDGMENT</u>
22.	DO <u>LEARN</u>
26.	DO <u>LOVE YOURSELF</u>
27.	DO ACCEPT <u>PERSECUTION</u>
28.	DO <u>PERSEVERE</u>
30.	DO <u>PREPARE</u>/WATCH
32.	DO <u>REPENT</u>/RECONCILE
34.	DO BE A GOOD <u>SERVANT</u>/SLAVE
35.	DO PROPER <u>SPEECH</u>/THOUGHTS
40.	DON'T WORRY

THINGS

12.	DO ACT CONCERNING <u>END</u> TIMES
33.	DO REGARDING <u>SACRAMENTS</u>
38.	DO <u>TREAT THINGS</u> RESPECTFULLY